American Capitalism, 1945–2000

AMERICAN CAPITALISM, 1945–2000

Continuity and Change from Mass Production to the Information Society

Wyatt Wells

The American Ways Series

IVAN R. DEE   *Chicago*

Library of Congress Cataloging-in-Publication Data:
Wells, Wyatt C.
    American capitalism, 1945–2000 : continuity and change from mass production to the information society / Wyatt Wells.
        p. cm. — (American ways series)
    Includes bibliographical references and index.
    ISBN 1-56663-537-3 (cloth : alk. paper) — ISBN 1-56663-538-1 (pbk. : alk. paper)
        1. United States—Economic conditions—1945-. 2. United States—Economic policy. I. Title. II. Series.

HC106.5.W465 2003
330.973'092—dc21   2003043843

For my son, Chase

Contents

Acknowledgments

THIS BOOK REFLECTS fifteen years of thought and study about the economy of the United States. At some point during this time, almost all of my family, friends, and colleagues have contributed to my thinking on the subject. Staci Ford, Tom McCraw, Ann Wells, Barbara Wells, Charles Wells, and James Yetman reviewed drafts of the manuscript and made valuable suggestions. John Braeman and Ivan Dee not only gave me the opportunity to write this book but contributed to its contents with wise counsel. Finally, I wish to thank the staff and management of El Rey in Montgomery, Alabama, and the Pacific Coffee on Hollywood Road in Hong Kong, where I actually wrote most of this book.

W. W.

Montgomery, Alabama
April 2003

American Capitalism, 1945–2000

Introduction: The Paradox of American Capitalism

IN THE SECOND HALF of the twentieth century the American economy experienced extraordinary change. Between 1945 and 2000 employment increased two and a half times, and output quintupled. Established industries like steel and textiles gradually decayed as new ones such as computers blossomed. New products, technologies, and techniques continuously rendered old ones obsolete—a process that economist Joseph Schumpeter dubbed "creative destruction." Yet these transformations occurred within a stable framework that not only permitted change but in many ways promoted it.

Capitalism predominated. That is to say, private, profit-seeking enterprises provided most goods and services, employed most workers, and commercialized most innovations. This was true even in sectors that were regulated by the government or that supplied it. There were critics of the system, to be sure, but they failed to challenge it effectively. As a practical matter, economic policy and thought operated within the limits imposed by capitalism.

Although the nation's specific economic problems and programs changed over time, public debate about them ultimately returned to the question of the source of wealth. Liberals attributed the country's economic success chiefly to the social context: diligent workers, wise laws, rich markets, good infrastructure, and plentiful natural resources. Conservatives credited prosperity first and foremost to entrepreneurs, who devised new products or better ways to make and market established ones. These two attitudes dictated different approaches to economic issues. If wealth was the product of the social context, efforts to improve education, health care, and the like offered the best way to maintain and extend prosperity. Financing such programs with stiff taxes on companies and the wealthy merely returned to society what it had created. But if, as conservatives claimed, entrepreneurs actually created wealth, such policies could be destructive.

International policy rested on the assumption that the country's economic and political well-being demanded prosperity abroad. Weakness in the larger world economy would damage American industry, and economic hardship could breed political instability in other countries, something that rarely worked to Washington's advantage. Most U.S. government officials further believed that general prosperity required a relatively open international economic system, with few barriers to trade or investment and the free exchange of currencies.

1

The Postwar Boom

IN 1945, at the close of World War II, Americans still lived in the shadow of the Great Depression. The unprecedented economic collapse of the 1930s had traumatized a generation and raised doubts about the viability of American capitalism. Many Americans—perhaps a majority—expected the depression to resume once the war was over. But after 1945 the United States launched on an extraordinary boom that would last, with some fits and starts, into the 1970s. Still, the memory of hardship strongly influenced how Americans approached the postwar era.

THE ISSUE OF INVESTMENT

After a victorious war, Americans had good reason for both pessimism and optimism about the economic future. The United States enjoyed the world's strongest economy, accounting for as much as 40 percent of global production of goods and services. During the war the country's factories had equipped the largest military in history—more than twelve million servicemen—while funneling billions of dollars of weapons and materiel to its allies. Americans nevertheless enjoyed, by most calculations, the world's highest standard of living.

The experience of the Great Depression, however, cast doubt on the durability of prosperity. The U.S. economy had collapsed in the 1930s, and recovery had been painfully slow. In 1939 production was still no higher than it had been in 1929, and unemployment was well above 15 percent. The experience scarred millions who lost their savings, jobs, businesses, homes, or farms in the disaster. Chiefly because of huge defense orders, the economy grew 75 percent between 1940 and 1944, and unemployment disappeared. But could prosperity survive peace? In 1944 the military purchased about 35 percent of the country's output, or Gross Domestic Product (GDP). When these expenditures ceased, observers feared that the economy might well sink back into depression.

Everyone agreed on the need to avoid a postwar depression, but no consensus existed on how to do so. To a large degree, divisions reflected political cleavages created in the 1930s by President Franklin D. Roosevelt's New Deal reforms. These had rested on two assumptions. First, that the American economy was "mature," with limited opportunities for growth. As Roosevelt had declared in 1932, "Our task now is not discovery or exploitation of natural resources, or necessarily producing more goods. It is the soberer, less dramatic business of administering resources and plants already in hand." The second assumption was that economic markets were at best imperfect, creating imbalances between regions, classes, and industries that had produced the depression. For instance, the chronic oversupply of agricultural products during the 1920s had depressed prices and impoverished farmers, rendering them unable to purchase manufactured goods and thus forcing companies to idle factories. Only government action could remedy these problems. The New Deal regulated transportation and energy to guarantee "fair" prices, encouraged the organization of labor unions, created agricultural programs that limited output and raised farm prices, increased taxes on the wealthy, created Social Security to insure workers against destitution, established a minimum wage and a standard work week, inaugurated public works for the orderly development of natural resources, and instituted relief programs for the unemployed.

World War II raised doubts about these assumptions, even among supporters of the New Deal. First, it demonstrated that the U.S. economy could indeed grow substantially, refuting assertions that it was somehow "mature." Second, the war indicated that private enterprise would produce if buyers existed—the problem was to ensure demand. In this view, investment held priority. Capital spending had collapsed during the depression, with outlays for housing, commercial real estate, machinery, new plants, railroads, and the like falling a staggering 87 percent between 1929 and 1933. Most observers assumed that if consumer spending revived, investment would follow, and New Deal reforms had sought to raise the purchasing power of consumers. But despite success in increasing consumer demand, investment did not recover. In 1939 consumer spending was actually 10 percent greater than it had been in 1929, but investment was 15 percent below the 1929 level. During the war, military outlays had more than compensated for weak investment, but peacetime prosperity would require strong capital spending.

This understanding led supporters of the New Deal—liberals—to gravitate to the theories of the British economist John Maynard Keynes. Traditionally economists had believed that the volume of savings determined investment. Companies and individuals borrowed idle funds to build houses, factories, railroads, and the like. An increase in the quantity of savings would lead to lower interest rates, and cheaper money would encourage more investment. Likewise, a shortage of savings would push interest rates up, restricting capital spending. Keynes, writing in the 1930s in response to the depression, reversed this formula, arguing that the level of investment determined the amount of savings. He contended that businessmen's expectations of the future

determined investment, with optimism encouraging capital
spending and pessimism deterring it. Interest rates were at most
a subordinate issue, because firms would not invest unless they
anticipated profit. If for some reason businessmen became pessimistic, they might well reduce capital spending below available
savings. Idle savings meant that the country was producing more
than it consumed, which would force business to reduce output.
Lower output meant lower employment and income, which of
course meant lower savings. Eventually the level of savings
would fall to that of investment, and production would stabilize.
At this point, however, the economy would have idle capacity,
substantial unemployment, and no immediate prospect of improvement.

Keynes argued that government policy should encourage
spending, not saving, relying on public investment financed by
government borrowing. A corollary was that such spending
would have disproportionate impact because of the "multiplier."
Keynes reasoned that those employed on public works would
save part of their income and spend the rest on food, clothing,
and the like, and that their outlays would wind up in the hands
of others. These people would, in turn, spend most of their income, and so on. Moreover, higher income would increase the
volume of savings and thus provide capital to finance public
investment.

In the late 1930s and early 1940s Keynes's ideas found increasing acceptance among American liberals and economists in general. They realized that the New Deal had not secured recovery
and that the Englishman's theories helped explain both the depression and the wartime boom. Alvin Hansen, a professor of
economics at Harvard, wedded Keynes's ideas to the theory of
industrial "maturity" common among reformers. He argued that
the Great Depression reflected a long-term decline in investment
opportunities in the United States. For 150 years, Hansen said,

the settlement of the frontier, the growth of the population, and the development of new technology had offered Americans extraordinary opportunities for profitable investment, guaranteeing prosperity. By the 1930s, however, the continent was settled and population growth was slowing. Technological advance alone was insufficient to keep investment strong. Only government spending on schools, public housing, roads, and the like could avoid stagnation. Hansen went further, however, arguing that public investment was in fact superior to the private variety. He wrote, "I am convinced that we could raise our total productivity more by a $20 billion public investment program than we could by a $20 billion private investment program, and the public investment program would, moreover, have the effect of enlarging very greatly the area of profitable private investment."

The Full Employment Act, introduced in Congress in early 1945, embodied these assumptions. It called for "a general program of such federal investment . . . sufficient to bring the aggregate volume of investment and expenditures by private business, consumers, and state and local governments and federal government, up to the level required to assure . . . full employment." To this end the bill would create a bureau to calculate the shortfall of private investment and to recommend compensatory spending projects to the president and Congress.

Conservatives associated with both the business community and the Republican party opposed ambitious plans for public investment. They had bitterly resented Roosevelt's New Deal reforms, which they believed worked against the interests of business. Higher taxes, the growth of organized labor, and a welter of regulations had reduced companies' autonomy and, in many cases, their income. Nor had Roosevelt's sometimes extravagant rhetorical attacks on big business—whose leaders he once labeled "economic royalists"—helped matters. Conservatives agreed that investment was vital, but they attributed anemic capital spending during the depression not to a lack of opportunities for profitable investment but to misguided government policy. Alfred Sloan, president of General Motors (GM), declared that economic stagnation reflected "political attacks on enterprise . . . [and] national economic policies that limited in large part the essential incentive for the normal development of enterprise with expanding job opportunities."

Many conservatives predicted that consumer spending and private investment would boom after the war, provided the government did not forestall it. Thomas E. Dewey, the Republican presidential nominee in 1944, noted that wartime shortages and rationing had created a huge backlog of consumer demand—in particular, the country had produced no automobiles for the civilian market during the war—even as full employment had allowed workers to save. The combination of available money and unmet needs, Dewey asserted, would keep American factories busy once the war was over, and buoyant demand would encourage investment. Alfred Sloan agreed: "Capital goods in large volume will be needed [after the war] not only for new production but to offset the obsolescence accumulated during the war," and he added that GM planned to spend a hefty $500 million on new products and facilities once peace returned.

Conservatives denied that public investment was somehow superior to the private variety. Public money, they argued, followed political influence and not necessarily the best economic or social return. Moreover, federal borrowing might well "crowd out" capital spending by business, consuming money that industry would otherwise have put into new plant and products. Public works could have value, but the government should fund these on their own merits, not as part of a general economic stabilization program, and the money should come from taxes, not borrowing.

Some thoughtful businessmen associated with the Committee

for Economic Development (CED), a private "think tank," demonstrated a limited acceptance of Keynes's theories. They argued that Washington should set its budget to yield a surplus when the economy was prosperous. Should a recession develop, tax revenue would fall, creating a deficit, which would stimulate demand and facilitate recovery. This approach would also allow the federal government to plan spending over the long run rather than having to change outlays with shifts in economic performance. It assumed, however, that private investment was basically strong and that government needed only to mitigate its inevitable fluctuations, not supplant it.

The CED's plan had the added advantage of addressing the business cycle, a problem too often overlooked in the debate over postwar economic policy. Since the Industrial Revolution in the eighteenth century, capitalist economies had experienced a recurring cycle of boom and bust. During a boom, rising prices and interest rates conspire with shortages to choke off expansion, creating recession. During a recession, falling prices and interest rates lay the foundation for a new boom. This pattern, which experience suggests is inherent to industrial capitalism, is a separate issue from long-term stagnation, the problem of the 1930s. The CED's prescription promised to mitigate the business cycle, which in the postwar era would be a far more pressing issue than stagnation.

The Employment Act, which Congress passed in 1946, embodied a "wait and see" attitude. It created a three-person Council of Economic Advisers (CEA) to make recommendations to the president, and it committed the government "to promote maximum employment, production, and purchasing power." But the bill said nothing about how the country should achieve these goals. For the moment, Congress seemed willing to see if private investment would materialize.

PLANNING A NEW WORLD ORDER

International policy occasioned less debate in Washington. World trade and finance had collapsed in the 1930s, and most economists and government officials believed that this breakdown had contributed mightily to the Great Depression. Economic hardship, in turn, had allowed militarists in Japan and Nazis in Germany to seize power in their countries and initiate World War II. This experience convinced most policymakers that, as Henry Morgenthau, Roosevelt's secretary of the Treasury, put it, "Economic stability . . . is indispensable for the maintenance of political stability."

Economic stability required that the world avoid the errors made after World War I. Then, the victors had made no coordinated effort to repair the disruptions of war, in particular the tangle of wartime debts and reparations that made the resumption of orderly international finance impossible. Instead governments sought to aid domestic producers against foreign competition, raising barriers to imports and manipulating their currencies to encourage exports and discourage purchases from abroad. Unfortunately, such measures encouraged retaliation, creating a cycle of restriction that sharply reduced the total volume of world trade.

Determined to avoid the mistakes of the past, American officials laid plans for an open system of trade and finance. Their plan called for governments to reduce trade barriers and apply them equally to other countries, renouncing the discrimination between different nations common before 1939. Governments would also stabilize their currencies, guaranteeing their value against and convertibility into the money of other countries. These changes would greatly promote international trade, ideally converting it from a source of weakness into an engine of growth.

In 1945 reality fell far short of this ideal. During the war every major country including the United States had strictly regulated trade, and these controls persisted into the postwar era. The United States was unusual in emerging richer from the war; most other major combatants had suffered severe and in many cases catastrophic economic losses. Reconstruction required governments to ration scarce foreign currency, making sure that it went for necessary products. American officials realized that, in light of the grim short-term outlook, their objectives required an agreement establishing an open system as the ultimate goal of the international economy. Otherwise, controls used to manage the immediate problems of reconstruction would become permanent.

At a 1944 conference at Bretton Woods, New Hampshire, the Allies had agreed on a new system of international finance. Finance received priority because without it trade cannot move—somehow people must pay for goods and services. Moreover, postwar reconstruction would impose heavy financial burdens, and most countries wanted a system to manage these in place quickly. The dollar would be the focus of the new regime. The United States would continue to value its currency at $35 to an ounce of gold, using the precious metal to redeem dollars held by other governments on demand. Other countries would "peg" their currencies to the greenback, buying and selling in financial markets to maintain the value of their money against the dollar. Countries could change their peg, but only in consultation with international authorities. Two supranational institutions would oversee this system: the International Monetary Fund (IMF) and the International Bank for Reconstruction and Development (IBRD, or World Bank). The IMF would have $8.8 billion in resources provided by members (including $3.25 billion from the United States) and would make short-term loans to countries that found themselves in financial difficulties. Members of the IMF, who included most countries of the United Nations, could draw small credits automatically, but the Fund could impose conditions on larger loans, requiring changes in the economic policies of recipients. The IMF would also set rules for international finance, approving changes in currency pegs and deciding when governments could impose controls on foreign exchange. The World Bank would provide long-term loans, initially for postwar reconstruction and then for economic development. It would have its own capital, provided by member countries, and would also secure funds by selling bonds in money markets like New York and London. Experts estimated that the IBRD's initial lending power would be about $3.2 billion.

Trade policy developed less rapidly. Although governments wanted a framework for finance in place when the war ended, most preferred to see how the postwar economy developed before committing to a new regime for trade. Nevertheless the American government began work on reducing trade barriers. In 1945 Congress granted the administration authority to cut tariffs by as much as 50 percent as part of a general agreement liberalizing trade. And in the months immediately after the war, Washington and London announced their support for the creation of a new supranational body, the International Trade Organization (ITO), which would set rules for trade, much as the IMF would for finance.

Everyone realized, however, that the IMF, the World Bank, and the ITO could not meet immediate postwar needs. None were in operation when the war ended, and even had they been, their resources were insufficient for the giant task of reconstruction. Fighting had severely damaged the industrial centers of Europe and East Asia, and the expense of war had bankrupted most of the countries involved. Among the great powers, only the United States had emerged from the war with a larger, more efficient industrial plant, and other countries planned to draw supplies for reconstruction from it. Anticipating this, the United States made provisions through the United Nations for $2.7 billion in food, fuel, and clothing to those rendered destitute by the war. It also loaned $3.5 billion to European governments to finance imports from the United States and granted the British government a special $3.75 billion credit. Ideally this money—almost $10 billion—would allow other countries to begin rebuilding and implementing open trade and financial policies.

RECONVERSION

Victory in August 1945 surprised most Americans. Germany collapsed more or less on schedule in May, but few expected Japan to surrender before the invasion of its home islands, which was not expected until the end of the year. Atomic bomb attacks on Japan in August brought the conflict to an abrupt end. Instead of an orderly reduction in military spending during the second half of 1945, Washington canceled billions of dollars' worth of defense contracts, throwing millions of people out of work. Meanwhile, managers scrambled to convert their plants from military to civilian production.

Contrary to the fears of many Americans, peace did not bring a new depression. During the war, workers had enjoyed high incomes even as wartime shortages and rationing had limited what they could buy. They had saved their money, and victory brought a huge leap in spending as consumers rushed to purchase clothes, appliances, automobiles, and other goods. Companies making these products hired those workers laid off from defense plants as well as demobilized servicemen. By 1946 total employment was greater than its wartime peak, and unemployment was a low

3.9 percent. Gross Domestic Product did decline in the wake of demobilization, falling 14 percent between 1945 and 1947, but this reflected extraordinary wartime conditions rather than weakness in the postwar economy.

Inflation, not unemployment, constituted the chief economic problem of reconversion. Washington had financed the war in large part by expanding the money supply—in effect, printing up currency. Normally, with more cash, individuals and firms spend more, bidding up prices and wages. To avoid this, the American government had during the war devised a complex system of controls to regulate wages and prices and to ration scarce materials like sugar and gasoline. President Harry S. Truman, who became chief executive after Roosevelt died in April 1945, planned to maintain controls into the immediate postwar era. The reconversion of factories to civilian production would take time, and in the interim there would be acute shortages of consumer goods and the danger that buyers, flush with cash, would bid prices up. The president warned that sharp price increases could be "the beginning of an inevitable spiral of uncontrolled inflation—a race between rising wages and rising prices" that only a deep recession could break. In particular the administration feared repeating the events that had occurred after World War I, when rapid price increases in 1919 had created conditions for a severe recession in 1920. Wage and price controls, it was hoped, would carry the nation through this period without disruption.

Soon after victory over Japan, however, Truman suggested that wages might rise, provided that employers did not pass on increases to consumers in the form of higher prices. Labor unions seized this opportunity, demanding wage hikes of as much as 30 percent, which they insisted companies could pay without raising their charges. Employers balked, declaring that they could not absorb such a huge increase in their costs without price hikes. Unions struck, and by early 1946, 200,000 auto workers, 300,000 meat packers, 180,000 electrical workers, and 750,000 steel workers were idle. Labor unrest significantly slowed reconversion—the fewer workers on the job, the fewer goods factories could produce for consumers. Strikes also gave other groups an excuse to ignore controls. For some items, like gasoline and meat, black markets grew dramatically; in other sectors, like automobiles, dealers demanded kickbacks to arrange sales; many small retailers simply ignored controls, knowing that the government did not have sufficient personnel to monitor them; and some producers, such as ranchers, held goods from the market in anticipation of higher prices.

By early 1946 controls were unraveling. To shore them up, Truman asked Congress to extend his authority to impose controls for another year, to July 1947. In the late spring of 1946 the legislature did extend price controls, but the bill granted exemptions or concessions to a great many industries. The president considered this measure useless and vetoed it. Controls ended, prices leaped forward, and a few weeks later Truman signed a bill similar to the one he had just vetoed. As he had warned, however, the measure proved unworkable, and the president lifted the remaining controls during the winter of 1946–1947. His poor handling of controls contributed mightily to Republican success in the 1946 elections, which gave the GOP control of Congress for the first time since 1930.

Fortunately the disasters predicted by Truman did not materialize. Striking unions settled for wage increases that averaged about 18 percent, which employers generally passed on to consumers in the form of higher prices. Between 1945 and 1948 prices increased by a third, which was perhaps inevitable in light of the substantial wartime expansion of the money supply. But prices stabilized in 1948. Industry returned to full civilian production, the backlog of consumer demand from the war exhausted itself, and Washington refrained from further expanding the money supply. No doubt the government could have handled the situation better, but the American economy was strong enough to absorb the shock of reconversion without permanent damage.

These events did have a lasting impact in one area, however: labor relations. Strikes encouraged revisions of the labor laws and led to an implicit settlement that defined the role of unions in American industry for a generation. Since 1933 labor unions had gone from victory to victory, aided by federal legislation that encouraged workers to organize. Between 1933 and 1945 union membership grew from two million to twelve million, with the portion of nonfarm workers belonging to unions increasing from 10 percent to 35 percent.

Some labor leaders—most notably Walter Reuther of the United Auto Workers (UAW)—hoped to secure a voice in management. When the UAW went on strike against GM in 1946, Reuther argued that the company could grant the union's demand for a 30 percent increase in wages without raising prices, and seemed to imply that the labor contract should contain a provision to that effect. GM refused to discuss the matter with the UAW. The company's leaders declared that, though they would negotiate wages and working conditions with organized labor— these were, after all, matters of intimate concern to union members—pricing was solely the responsibility of management. The company, they claimed, had a "right to manage" its own property. The strike dragged on for months, but in the face of corporate intransigence and popular impatience, the UAW gave up its demand for a role in management.

Instead of expanding the role of organized labor, postwar strikes encouraged a substantial revision of the labor laws. Because organized labor was the first major interest group to break with price controls, and because strikes hampered reconversion, unions received much of the blame for postwar inflation. In the 1946 elections, Republicans gained a majority in Congress in part by capitalizing on this sentiment, and the new Congress made reform of labor laws a priority. The result was the Taft-Hartley Act of 1948, which banned several "unfair" union tactics such as jurisdictional strikes and secondary boycotts. It also gave the president the authority to order striking workers back to their jobs for a ninety-day "cooling off" period if a labor dispute threatened national well-being. And it outlawed the "closed shop," under which companies agreed to hire only union members, and gave state governments the option of banning the "union shop," under which a newly hired worker had to join the union with which his or her employer had a contract.

Although labor leaders christened it the "slave labor" act, unions had little difficulty living with Taft-Hartley's requirements, and in time only the provision allowing states to ban the union shop remained controversial. But emotions ran high because, whereas New Deal–era legislation had arrayed the government behind organized labor, Taft-Hartley recast Washington as a neutral broker between labor and management.

A series of contracts between GM and the UAW in the late 1940s and early 1950s set the pattern for postwar labor relations, at least in heavy manufacturing industries like automobiles, steel, and rubber. GM agreed to raises of 2 percent a year plus the increase in consumer prices (a cost of living allowance, or COLA), and it made provisions for ever more generous health and retirement benefits. These contracts also spelled out in detail exactly what workers were supposed to do—how long they could work, when they could take breaks, and what tasks they could and could not perform.

This system received substantial criticism, particularly for its inflexibility. Agreements regulated work in ways that impeded productivity. For instance, contracts usually prohibited a worker

who operated a particular machine from repairing it if something went wrong. Managers could not move workers from one
area of a plant where work might be slack to another that was
busier without first consulting the union. More broadly, critics
argued that by concentrating so many decisions among the relative handful who negotiated a contract, this approach stifled the
initiative of workers, foremen, and managers on the shop floor.

Nevertheless this approach to labor relations yielded substantial benefits. It brought peace to factories after years of conflict
between management and labor. It gave workers high wages and
generous benefits that allowed millions of them to graduate to
the middle class. And these gains accrued without critically im-
pairing the growth of productivity in the 1950s and 1960s, when
output per worker expanded by a healthy 3 percent annually, fast
enough to finance both higher wages and larger profits.

The flaws in this approach to labor relations reflected an unpleasant but inescapable reality—labor and management in-
tensely distrusted each other. As a rule, American companies had
stubbornly resisted unions until the 1930s and early 1940s, when
huge strikes and government pressure had finally forced recognition. Organized labor had got what it had by confrontation,
not cooperation. Meanwhile the demands of Reuther and like-
minded unionists convinced management that organized labor
would, if it could, take control of their firms. Only precise, de-
tailed contracts that anticipated every contingency could allow
the two sides to work together smoothly.

In retrospect the mid-1940s represented the apex of organized
labor's influence in the United States. For the generation after
1945, union membership as a portion of the nonfarm labor force
remained steady at 35 percent, with the numbers of organized
labor growing only as fast as total employment. Although hardly
a disaster, this represented a big change from the rapid growth of
the 1930s and early 1940s. Several factors account for this relative

stagnation. By 1945 the heavy manufacturing industries, where union growth had been greatest, were largely organized; public opinion, which in the 1930s had supported organized labor, after 1945 became less enthusiastic and in many cases hostile; and finally, as they became more established, unions may have lost some of their militant edge. Organized labor remained a powerful interest group throughout the postwar era, but it ceased to be a great instrument for economic change.

POSTWAR RECONSTRUCTION ABROAD

In the late 1940s the United States made the economic rehabilitation of Western Europe and Japan a priority. A variety of motives guided policy. Before 1939 these countries had been the chief trading partners of the United States, and their recovery would strengthen the U.S. economy. Diplomatic concerns, however, were more important than economic ones. In the 1930s economic instability in Europe and Asia had led to political unrest and war. And in the late 1940s U.S. officials were increasingly concerned about the ambitions of the Soviet Union, which had imposed Communist governments on the countries of Eastern Europe and largely sealed them off from outside influence. Washington saw stable, prosperous, democratic regimes in Western Europe and Japan as bulwarks against Soviet expansion.

Western Europe had substantial economic problems. Before 1939 it had purchased raw materials from Eastern Europe and capital goods from Germany, selling consumer products in exchange. After 1945 the Soviet occupation of Eastern Europe sharply reduced trade with countries there, and Germany was a wreck, unable to import or export much. American farms and factories could make good the deficit of raw materials and capital goods, but the countries of Western Europe lacked the dollars with which to buy. The war had disrupted their export markets, in some cases permanently, and many Europeans had lost investment abroad that had, before the war, served as a major source of foreign currency to pay for imports. Finally, Western Europe had suffered considerable physical damage during the war. Plans to remedy long-term deficiencies sometimes exacerbated short-term ones. After 1945 several Western European countries launched ambitious programs to modernize and expand industries damaged by six years of war and ten years of depression, putting the emphasis on heavy industry (steel, cement, electricity, machinery, and the like). These efforts increased the demand for capital goods that only the United States could provide. In 1946 the United States had a current account surplus of almost $5 billion, a figure that swelled to nearly $9 billion in 1947. The $10 billion in aid and loans provided by the American government immediately after the war to finance reconstruction, which had seemed so generous at the time, was quickly exhausted.

An economic crisis in Britain in the summer of 1947 forced the United States to launch a new initiative. As a condition of its $3.75 billion loan, Washington had required that London make the pound sterling convertible into dollars by the summer of 1947, scrapping most controls on foreign exchange. But as the deadline approached, it was clear that Britain's current account deficit with the United States was increasing, casting doubt on the stability of the pound. The advent of convertibility led to a run on sterling as holders sold it for dollars. Britain lost $1.05 billion over seven weeks in the summer of 1947, exhausting its dollar reserves and forcing it to suspend convertibility. America's chief ally, the recipient of its most generous financial assistance, and Europe's strongest economy—Britain—was on the verge of bankruptcy, and it was clear that the rest of Western Europe was in no better shape.

European bankruptcy would have had several unpleasant implications. First, American exports would have dropped sharply, although in light of the boom under way in the United States, this probably would not have been disastrous. Still, those sectors that depended on exports, like agriculture, would undoubtedly have suffered. More important, if Europe ran out of dollars, its governments would have to scale back or abandon altogether plans for industrial modernization as well as impose strict controls on imports and foreign exchange. The former would create a severe recession in Europe; the latter would delay indefinitely the inauguration of the open economic system that the United States sought to build. American officials feared the ramifications of both. Recession would further destabilize the politics of Western Europe, raising the possibility that Communists might take control of governments, particularly in France and Italy where their parties were quite strong. And American officials believed that, in the long run, a system of open markets and stable currencies offered the best environment for economic growth, which was not only good in and of itself but also reinforced political stability.

To deal with the crisis, Secretary of State General George Marshall in 1947 announced $12 billion in grants (not loans) to European countries over the next four years. The money, known as the Marshall Plan, came with the condition that European countries work together to coordinate recovery. This aid staved off the immediate crisis. Grants allowed countries to finance imports and so gave them more time to modernize industry, strengthening their capacity both to serve domestic markets and to export. To make dollars go as far as possible, European governments strictly rationed them, limiting imports from the United States to vital goods and, where possible, obtaining supplies from countries that did not demand dollars in payment. Although condoning such measures, the Marshall Plan made clear that they were temporary, to be abandoned as soon as conditions improved.

The permanent resolution of Europe's economic problems, however, entailed major reforms. In 1949 the countries of Western Europe created a payments union. Before this time, trade had rested on bilateral currency agreements. For example, France and Belgium had constantly balanced the receipts from imports and exports, and if one accumulated a large deficit, it would sharply limit imports from the other. The new payments union was far more flexible. If France had a surplus with Italy but a deficit with Belgium, it could use its credits with Italy to pay Belgium. This made it much easier for Europeans to supply their own needs. The countries of Western Europe also devalued their currencies by 20 to 30 percent against the dollar, with the British pound, the most important, going from $4.00 to $2.80. This step made European exports cheaper and imports more expensive, encouraging the former and retarding the latter.

The most dramatic initiative involved the economic rehabilitation of West Germany. Before the war, Germany had been Europe's largest economy. After 1945 the Allies had occupied it, with each taking a designated zone. Initially they planned to restrict German industry so that the country could never again make war. Starting in 1948, however, the Western Allies, led by the United States, implemented a recovery plan for their zones of Germany, the area that would become West Germany. They replaced the virtually worthless Reichsmark with a new currency, the deutschemark, and German authorities themselves scrapped the complex system of price controls and rationing inherited from the Nazis. Production rebounded sharply, and as output rose the Allies gradually abandoned restrictions on industrial production. The revival of German industry vastly increased the capacity of the European economy as a whole, providing goods like coal, machinery, and steel previously in short supply and adding to the continent's export potential.

The creation of the European Coal and Steel Community

(ECSC) in 1950 further advanced the process of reform and opened new political possibilities for the continent. Chronic shortages of coal and disputes about the future of the steel industry threatened economic recovery and led the French government to propose a united market for these two products as well as the establishment of a single, supranational authority to coordinate the badly needed modernization of mines and mills. West Germany, Italy, Belgium, the Netherlands, and Luxembourg quickly accepted the French plan. The United States supported the effort, not only diplomatically but also with low-interest loans to finance modernization. The ECSC proved a great success, allowing higher production at lower cost. In 1957 its members expanded on this example, signing a broad pact abolishing all barriers to trade between themselves, thereby creating the European Community, the forerunner of the European Union (EU). By this time Western Europe had fully recovered from the war and had begun a sustained boom at least as impressive as that under way in the United States.

The United States also supported Japan's recovery, albeit on a smaller scale. After the war the American military occupied Japan, governing it until 1952 when control returned to an elected Japanese government. Postwar conditions in Japan were even worse than in Europe. The war had physically devastated the country and had terminated almost all its foreign trade—and Japan had always imported most of its raw materials and much of its food. At first, occupation authorities pursued an uncertain economic policy because, as with Germany, many American officials desired permanent restrictions on Japanese industry to limit the country's military potential. In 1948, however, occupation authorities imposed a comprehensive recovery program: balancing the budget, fixing the value of the yen against the dollar, and creating a revolving fund to pay for imports of raw materials such as cotton that Japanese industry would process and reexport. The

outbreak of war in Korea in 1950 provided another boost because
the American military procured many supplies in Japan, which
was convenient to the front. By the late 1950s Japan had em-
barked on an extraordinary boom, with production more than
quadrupling between 1958 and 1973.

Although the recovery of Europe and Japan owed chiefly to
the hard work and ingenuity of the people there, the United
States provided important assistance. It not only helped finance
the process but lent important diplomatic support to initiatives
like the European payments union and the ECSC. This effort allowed the revival of the chief foreign competitors of U.S. industry, which would in time have important consequences. But the
economic revival of Western Europe and Japan yielded great political advantages. U.S. officials also operated on the assumption
that great imbalances in the world economy, such as existed immediately after 1945, were dangerous. The American economy
did not exist in isolation but as part of a larger whole, and its
well-being was ultimately tied to that of the broader system.

Throughout reconstruction the United States proceeded with
plans to create an open world economy. In 1947 a conference involving most of the leading trading nations agreed on the General Agreement on Tariffs and Trade (GATT), which cut tariffs
by almost half. Subsequent GATT "rounds" in the 1960s and
1970s reduced tariffs on most goods to negligible levels. The International Trade Organization fared less well. Tortuous negotiations in 1947 and 1948 produced an agreement, but it satisfied
few. The key issues were quotas on imports and foreign investment. The United States and Britain had sought to ban quotas
altogether and to provide guarantees for foreign investors. Developing countries, however, demanded the right to protect domestic industry against competition from abroad and to regulate
foreign investment in their countries. The final agreement com-
promised, offering general language denouncing quotas and de-

fending foreign investment, but in both cases providing a host of exceptions. The American Congress concluded that these exceptions would in fact institutionalize abuses and refused to ratify the agreement, killing it. In time GATT became the primary vehicle for reducing trade barriers.

The Bretton Woods accords fared better. By 1958 economic recovery in Western Europe had allowed countries there to implement most of the provisions of these agreements, stabilizing their currencies and allowing free conversion for current transactions—that is, trade in goods and services, tourism, and the payment of dividends on investments and interest on debts. Japan followed in the early 1960s. (Many of these countries did, however, by controlling capital movements, restrict the use of foreign exchange for investment abroad.) Throughout the postwar era, members regularly increased the capital of the IMF and the World Bank in line with the growth of the world economy. It took nearly fifteen years, but under GATT and Bretton Woods the industrial countries largely realized the ideal of an open world economy. Stable, convertible currencies and large reductions in trade barriers yielded the results Washington desired. Throughout the second half of the twentieth century, international trade expanded faster than total world production of goods and services, providing a great stimulus to growth. The process was not smooth, and exceptions were legion, but progress was nevertheless remarkable.

CONTOURS OF PROSPERITY

Prosperity was the dominant theme of the postwar era. In 1945 the United States launched into a boom that would, with a few minor interruptions, last until 1973. During these years Gross Domestic Product grew 140 percent and real (inflation-adjusted) per capita income doubled. Living standards improved to the point where the large majority of Americans could reasonably describe themselves as middle class.

Investment constituted the foundation of prosperity, performing two functions. First, capital spending kept demand strong, guaranteeing that the United States fully exploited available resources. Second and more important, capital spending expanded the country's economic resources. A growing population demanded housing, education, and employment, and living standards could improve only if productivity—output per worker—increased. These all required investment. Capital spending totaled $30 billion in 1946 and increased from there, throughout the postwar era constituting at least 15 percent of GDP.

Housing made up the single largest object of investment in the postwar era. Depression and war had discouraged construction, and the housing stock in the United States in 1945 was actually smaller than it had been in 1929. Americans responded energetically to this shortage. Before 1945 the United States had never built one million homes in a single year. After 1945 the United States never built fewer than one million homes a year. Construction centered in new suburbs. William Levitt, the most famous builder, developed suburbs of seventeen thousand homes each near New York and Philadelphia, using innovative mass-production techniques that sharply reduced costs. His employees operated in teams: the first surveyed roads and house lots, the next paved roads, the next laid foundations, the next erected frames, and so on, constructing thousands of identical homes. Levitt's houses may have lacked personality, but they were solid and comfortable and sold for less than $7,000. Activity centered in the suburbs because there developers could find relatively inexpensive tracts of land and employ their workers in teams, an impossibility in cramped urban sites. And many families now preferred suburbs to the cities because they could have a yard and in general enjoy more space.

The construction boom stimulated a vast array of related industries. Makers of concrete and cement, lumber, building equipment, and home appliances all profited. The migration to the suburbs also required the construction of sewers, roads, schools, and shopping centers to serve large populations in heretofore rural areas. Most notably, the automobile industry benefited. Suburbs required transportation—in contrast to cities, shops and schools were rarely within walking distance of homes. Two-car families became increasingly common, and three- and even four-car families were not unknown among those with teenage children. In the best prewar year, 1929, the United States had produced 4.5 million automobiles; in 1955 its factories turned out 7.9 million.

The government underwrote much of the housing boom. Washington insured long-term mortgages through the Federal Housing Authority (FHA) and the Veterans Administration, guaranteeing against default. This allowed lenders to grant twenty-, twenty-five-, and even thirty-year mortgages with confidence, whereas previously loans had rarely exceeded ten years. Longer terms permitted home buyers to stretch out repayment and thus keep their monthly mortgage bills low. The government created Savings & Loans (S&Ls) specifically to finance housing, allowing these institutions to pay savers slightly higher rates but requiring them to channel most of their funds into residential mortgages. The tax code also allowed homeowners to deduct the interest they paid on mortgages from their income for purposes of determining what they owed the government. In 1955 Washington provided another boost when it initiated construction of the interstate highway system, which by 1980 consisted of more than forty thousand miles of limited-access, high-speed roadways which not only connected the country's major cities to each other but also linked outlying suburbs with urban centers.

Washington also supported the economy through the GI Bill of Rights, which sought to integrate veterans smoothly back into society upon the war's end. It provided returning servicemen unemployment benefits, loans for the start of businesses and the purchase of homes, and, perhaps most important, money for veterans to attend college. Millions took advantage of this last benefit. Between 1940 and 1950 the number of Americans with college degrees increased by 50 percent, from six to nine million. The GI Bill represented a huge investment in human capital, equipping the population with valuable skills and knowledge.

Demography too played a role in the postwar boom. Between 1945 and 1965 American women had approximately eighty million babies. The country had to feed, clothe, house, and educate these youngsters, the fabled "baby boom" generation. The economic impact was substantial—for instance, between 1950 and 1970 enrollment in elementary and high schools grew from 27 million to 51 million, requiring the expansion of old schools and the construction of new ones.

Although the housing and baby booms guaranteed strong demand and high employment, they could not raise living standards in the long run. Only advances in worker productivity could accomplish this. Higher productivity entailed either the more efficient production of existing goods or the provision of new, better products. Between 1945 and 1973 output per worker grew at a healthy average of 3 percent a year, enough to double income in a generation.

In any economy, new industries exhibit the fastest growth. Television represented the first great postwar success, with the Radio Corporation of America (RCA) leading the way. The company's scientists and engineers had been working on TV technology since the 1920s, and the firm had begun to commercialize television in the late 1930s, but the war had halted the effort. Peace offered RCA another chance. In 1946 it sold only

10,000 TV sets, but the number mushroomed to 200,000 the next year. In 1948 the United States made 1 million sets, and two years later the number was 7.5 million. Of course, TV sets required programming. By 1950 the country had 100 television stations, and by 1960, 580 stations were broadcasting. RCA followed this triumph by introducing color television in 1954. Progress was slow, with sales becoming significant only after 1960. In 1965, however, Americans bought 5 million color TV sets. Probably no economic development after 1945, with the exception of the growth of computers and the Internet, so changed the daily lives of Americans and, eventually, people everywhere. Television absorbed several hours of viewers' lives each day, creating a stronger basis for a common culture and allowing people to see for themselves events anywhere in the world, or even in outer space.

Chemical companies exploited comparable opportunities. In the twenty years before 1945 scientists had learned how to convert petroleum into plastics that could take a wide variety of forms—fibers, glass, tiles, pipes, insulation, and many more. The war had delayed the introduction of these materials to consumers, but after 1945 American chemical companies offered one new product after another. For the next twenty-eight years the chemical industry grew two and a half times as fast as the economy as a whole, as cheap, durable plastics replaced a variety of other materials. For instance, by the 1980s synthetic fibers like nylon and polyester constituted 70 percent of all fibers woven into cloth in the United States.

The development of new industries carried a price. Television badly hurt the movie industry; the number of movie theaters, which peaked at more than twenty thousand in 1954, by 1970 declined to sixteen thousand. Synthetic fibers pushed out of business many of those who raised sheep or grew cotton. Nevertheless society as a whole benefited. To the degree that new industries displaced older ones, it was because they better pleased consumers. Nylon was cheaper and stronger than natural fibers, television more intimate and convenient than movie theaters. In economic terms, greater value for consumers represented higher productivity. Such gains were sometimes hard to quantify—exactly how much did consumers benefit from having televisions in their homes as opposed to a movie theater a few miles away? Still, the gains were substantial enough to form the basis of a huge new industry.

The pharmaceutical industry, which is closely related to chemicals, offered the most dramatic social gains. In the 1930s scientists had discovered penicillin, the first modern antibiotic, and it became available to Allied soldiers during the war. After 1945 drug companies offered it to the public at large, providing the first really effective treatment for a whole host of dangerous illnesses, from strep throat to pneumonia. In the 1940s and 1950s companies also developed and marketed vaccines that largely banished a variety of grave diseases, including whooping cough, diphtheria, and polio. While pharmaceutical firms profited greatly, consumers benefited even more. And because patents on drugs lasted only nineteen years, companies had to invest much of their earnings in research to find new drugs to replace those on which patents were expiring.

In general, postwar American industry invested heavily in research and development (R&D), searching for new products and better ways to make existing ones. Throughout the 1950s and 1960s R&D consumed about 2.6 percent of GDP. Companies provided a little less than half this sum; the government, which devoted its R&D efforts chiefly to defense and the space program, provided the other half. Most government-funded work, however, occurred in university or company laboratories. Calculating the exact return from this investment is difficult, but scientific discoveries made possible many of the country's economic advances.

Although television, plastics, and pharmaceuticals developed with only limited government help, two other rapidly growing sectors, computers and aerospace, depended heavily on Washington's patronage. The army financed the first electronic computer, built during World War II, but by the mid-1950s private companies, most notably International Business Machines (IBM), were offering firms like insurance companies such machines to manage their records. These computers were mainframes that cost as much as a million dollars and weighed several tons. Washington, however, remained the largest single consumer, purchasing machines not only for the military but also for bureaus like the Social Security Administration. The federal government also funded most of the research on electronics, though it relied on universities and private firms to carry out the work. In this hothouse atmosphere, companies grew fast, developing and bringing to market a great many new technologies. Fairchild Semiconductor and Texas Instruments (TI) developed the first integrated circuits in the late 1950s, and Intel and TI produced the first microprocessors in the late 1960s. Most notably, in the early 1960s IBM spent a staggering $5 billion of its own money to develop the revolutionary System 360, a flexible set of computers that could serve a variety of purposes—government, business, and academic—and could even communicate with each other. This breakthrough made IBM the dominant force in the computer industry, a position it would hold for thirty years.

The aerospace industry depended even more heavily on the federal government. It had expanded massively during World War II to supply the government with warplanes, but peace had led to sharp declines in orders. Airplane sales by Douglas, one of the industry's largest firms, plummeted from 11,500 in 1945 to

127 in 1946. The industry recovered only with rising military spending during the Korean War, and government orders remained strong throughout the rest of the cold war. In the 1960s Washington's space program provided another source of revenue.

Aerospace companies did apply to private markets the experience they had gained working for the military. Boeing's 707 jetliners, introduced in the mid-1950s, drew heavily from the bombers it made for the air force and greatly increased the speed and safety of air travel. Eventually the civilian market rivaled the military one for manufacturers. Only 3.2 million passengers traveled by air in 1940, but 58 million did in 1960, and the number climbed to 297 million in 1980.

What impact did military spending have on the companies involved and on the economy as a whole? Critics of American capitalism have argued that defense outlays kept an otherwise stagnant economy expanding but weakened it in the long run by leading companies to concentrate on production for the government while neglecting consumer and foreign markets. The first of these arguments is not particularly strong. Military spending certainly did stimulate the economy, but in most cases high taxes financed outlays, so that the net effect was probably not great over the long term. Had Washington spent 4 to 5 percent of GDP on the military in the 1950s and 1960s, rather than 8 to 10 percent, it could have lowered taxes and interest rates substantially, stimulating the economy that way. Moreover, inflation was a threat during much of the postwar era, suggesting that the economy could have done with less stimulus.

The second argument is more problematic. Military research and the space program did occupy huge numbers of engineers and scientists who otherwise would have been available for commercial projects. But it is impossible to know how many of these people private industry could have absorbed, or how many the cold war or the space program inspired to become scientists or engineers in the first place. Military demands may have distracted some companies from commercial opportunities (this seems to have been one of RCA's problems in the 1960s and 1970s). But firms like Boeing used technologies developed for the military in civilian markets, and companies like IBM could spend so heavily on research in part because their managers knew that the government would buy a large portion of whatever they developed. Military spending did alter the contours of the U.S. economy, for instance encouraging aerospace at the expense of consumer products. But it is not clear that the result was a smaller or less productive economy overall.

The debate over the economic effects of defense spending often misses the point. The proper question is not, "How did military spending affect growth?" but "How much did the country need to spend on defense?" If military expenditures substantially increased the security of the United States, they were worth somewhat lower growth. If defense spending did not improve security, the country certainly could have found better uses for the money.

Throughout the postwar era, established American industries invested heavily to improve the productivity of workers. In some cases new, improved machinery increased output per worker. New alloys allowed machine tools to cut metal faster and more accurately. Just as often, however, new methods of organization accounted for advances. In the 1960s and 1970s shippers increasingly packed their goods at the point of origin in large steel containers that fit on trucks, railroad cars, and, most important, ships. These containers remained closed until they reached their final destination, moving by crane from one form of transport to another, thereby eliminating the need to repack cargo at each step of its journey. As a consequence, between 1950 and 1970 the number of longshoremen declined from 73,000 to 47,000 even though traffic more than doubled. Usually, however, new technology and changes in organization went together. Starting in the 1950s, insurance companies, government bureaus, banks, payroll offices, and similar organizations moved their records from paper to computers, vastly improving the rate at which they could store, access, and update information. This required not only new machinery but also the retraining of office workers.

The most dramatic increases in manufacturing productivity came from the construction of automated, "green-field" factories in the countryside that wedded new technology with new organization. Since the late nineteenth century, American companies had increasingly relied on mass production. They standardized the design of their goods, broke production down into its various components, assigned each worker a specific task in the process, and arranged workers on some sort of assembly line. The result was a huge number of cheap, identical products. Chicago's stockyards and Henry Ford's automobile plants were classic examples of mass production. Yet before 1945, in order to secure workers, companies had to locate in urban areas, and their plants had to conform to the limits of available real estate. As a result, factories often stretched over several floors and even included noncontiguous buildings. Less-than-optimal layouts limited efficiency. The growth of suburbs and expanding automobile ownership freed companies from urban sites, allowing them to construct plants in the countryside—"green fields"—with layouts that allowed maximum productivity.

Other factors, secondary to efficiency but still important, encouraged the development of new facilities in the countryside. Land was cheap, at least compared with that in cities. Local governments were accommodating, often providing companies with tax concessions or free services. And workers, usually from small towns or farms, were generally suspicious of labor unions. In many cases large firms managed to keep organized labor out of new rural plants even while accommodating it in old urban ones. Pay and benefits were usually the same at both types of plants, but companies did not have to negotiate work rules at nonunion factories, an important matter since reorganization of the labor force was often central to improved productivity.

Green-field plants could yield dramatic increases in productivity. For instance, in the 1950s Timken, the nation's leading maker of bearings, constructed a new factory that made standardized bearings using automated, continuous-processing technology at Bucyrus, Ohio, a town of about twelve thousand. By the end of the decade Timken was able to sell bearings from Bucyrus at 15 to 25 percent less than identical products from other Timken plants, even while enjoying larger profit margins on them.

The shift of manufacturing from urban to previously rural sites had a major negative impact on cities. Employment opportunities in urban centers declined, particularly for unskilled workers. In 1964 the journalist Theodore H. White wrote, "In Chicago, erstwhile 'hog butcher for the world,' the packing houses once employed 20,000 workers. . . . Today Chicago no longer butchers hogs for the world, for the packers have moved to new and more efficient plants elsewhere, and their South Side workers will never be employed again." Displaced workers had to move to the suburbs or find new jobs that often did not pay as well as the old. This shift greatly contributed to the decline of urban neighborhoods in the postwar era despite concerted efforts by local, state, and national authorities to halt the deterioration of central cities.

Mass production entailed more than green-field plants, however. As the management expert Peter Drucker wrote in 1946, "Any operation can be handled by modern mass production methods if the volume is only large enough." Levitt used mass-production techniques to build houses, McDonald's to cook burgers and fries. To the degree that American industry had an ideology of production in the 1940s and 1950s, it was mass production. Exceptions existed—Boeing built planes to order because the market was not large enough to support mass production. Nevertheless many of the most dynamic American companies owed their success to the effective application of mass-production techniques.

New managerial techniques complemented improvements in technology and organization. Between 1900 and 1930 DuPont and General Motors had developed sophisticated accounting practices that allowed them to track closely their costs and return on investment. Such knowledge may seem elementary, but for large and many medium-sized companies, with hundreds and even thousands of employees scattered over many locations, it was difficult to obtain. After 1945 these techniques became standard in American business, allowing managers to make better-informed decisions.

New corporate structures further improved the quality of management. Traditionally most large American companies had organized themselves functionally—that is, one department handled manufacturing, another marketing, another purchasing, and so on. This approach had two drawbacks. First, middle managers had no perspective on the company as a whole. For instance, those in marketing had little knowledge of problems in manufacturing that might affect sales. Second, if a company handled a variety of products, managers might end up making and selling several entirely different products, a difficult situation for even the most talented executives. In the 1920s and 1930s a handful of American companies—most notably DuPont, GM, Sears, and Standard Oil (Exxon)—had confronted these problems and devised a solution: the multi-divisional organization. They reorganized themselves along product or regional lines, with each division handling all aspects of business for a particular good or area. At DuPont, for example, a single executive oversaw the making and marketing of paint. This task was manageable, and it allowed executives to coordinate various aspects of the business like sales and production. It made the evaluation of different lines of business easier. The multi-divisional organization also permitted chief corporate officers to concentrate on the future direction of the business instead of the day-to-day coordination of departments. After 1945 the multi-divisional form of organization gradually became standard for most large American firms making more than one kind of product.

Improvements in marketing also yielded substantial advances. The use of surveys, focus groups, and other devices pioneered before World War II by firms like Procter & Gamble allowed companies to launch new products and sell old ones with greater confidence. Marketing remained as much an art as a science—most new products and advertising campaigns actually failed to sway consumers—but the new techniques did reduce the number of false starts and the waste of resources associated with them.

The most extraordinary productivity gains came not in manufacturing, services, or construction, but in agriculture. In the mid-1930s the Roosevelt administration had imposed a system of government-guaranteed price supports coupled with mandatory limits on planting designed to prop up farm prices and income. The tremendous productivity of American agriculture created constant difficulties for these programs. Except during World War II and its immediate aftermath, supply outran demand. To keep prices stable, the government had to buy the surplus, either storing it in the hope that in the future stronger demand would allow its orderly sale, or dumping it at low prices on world markets, disrupting them and creating a large loss for Washington.

Farm programs, however, expedited an extraordinary advance in farm productivity. In 1940 almost 10 million Americans worked the land. New Deal agricultural programs sought, by stabilizing prices, to rescue this group from poverty. Instead, restrictions on planting drove many tenants and sharecroppers from the land because, with fields idle, landlords no longer needed them. Guaranteed prices made it easier for farmers, confident of the earnings from their crops, to invest in tractors, reapers, and cotton pickers as well as to buy expensive chemical fertilizers, pesticides, and herbicides. Such expenditures vastly increased both output per acre and the amount of land one person could farm. Only better-off farmers could fully exploit these technologies, however. Tractors and reapers operated best on large tracts of land, and machinery and chemicals required financing most readily available to those with substantial property. As a result the countryside emptied out after 1945, even as farm production broke records. In 1960 only about 5 million Americans still worked the land, and by 1990 the number was down to a little more than 3 million. Between 1950 and 1980 the size of the average farm grew from 200 to 400 acres. Meanwhile, between 1945 and 1980 the amount of wheat produced in the United States grew from a little over a billion bushels to 2.3 billion, and the corn harvest expanded from 2.5 billion bushels to 6.6 billion.

This change entailed huge social disruption, particularly in the South where before 1945 agriculture had been particularly labor intensive. Millions had to uproot themselves, and small towns across the country that had flourished for decades wilted. But however painful, there is no doubt that change was, on balance, beneficial to the nation. Americans got plentiful food at reasonable prices, while those displaced from the land generally found work in sectors where productivity was not growing as fast. Displaced farm workers frequently improved their standard of living—despite the wholesome aura that attaches to rural life, the existence of a factory worker is usually far superior to that of a sharecropper.

THE ECONOMICS OF REFORM

The Truman administration saw itself as the continuation of the New Deal. It doubted the capacity of private enterprise to deal with social problems—Washington had to intervene, making public investments and regulating markets in the general interest. But the context differed from the 1930s. The economy was prosperous, making massive recovery programs unnecessary, while good times disinclined the public from radical change. Why, people reasoned, reform an economy that already provided jobs and a high and rising standard of living? Congress was evenly divided between Republicans and Democrats, and on economic issues the large contingent of Democrats from the South were almost as conservative as their Republican brethren. As a result, the passage of controversial programs was difficult. Finally, the developing cold war forced Truman and his chief advisers to devote much of their attention to foreign affairs.

Financial concerns also encouraged caution. Washington had paid about half the expense of World War II by borrowing, and in 1945 the federal government owed $270 billion, the equivalent of 121 percent of GDP. This last figure is probably the best measure of the actual burden imposed by government debt on an economy because it relates the size of debt to the resources available to service it. In 1945 it was the highest in U.S. history. Inflation constituted the chief domestic economic problem facing Truman's administration, and the president believed, along with most economists, that government deficits fed rising prices by stoking the demand for goods and services. (A deficit meant that Washington was adding more to demand in the form of spending than it was taking out in taxes.) Balanced budgets or, even better, surpluses were among the best weapons against rising prices. The Truman administration ran a surplus during four of its eight years in office and managed to keep its four deficits small. When Truman left office, the federal debt was still $270 billion, but because the economy had grown and prices had risen, that figure represented 71 percent of GDP.

In retrospect, Truman's aversion to deficits was wise. The country was prosperous during most of his tenure, with strong private investment, making government investment financed by borrowing unnecessary. During the relatively mild recession of 1949, the Truman administration kept spending steady even as revenue fell, and so ran a deficit that provided some economic stimulus. Meanwhile a tax cut authorized by Congress in 1948 took effect, putting more money into the hands of consumers and business. The strong economic recovery of 1950 justified this cautious policy and, incidentally, returned the government to surplus as tax revenues expanded with GDP.

Despite his commitment to balanced budgets, Truman strongly supported public investment. But he recommended programs not to stimulate the economy but to address pressing social needs. The president urged the construction of public housing for the poor, aid to local school districts facing rising enrollments, and the creation of regional authorities to develop water power. The Tennessee Valley Authority (TVA), a New Deal showcase that had constructed twenty-two dams along the Tennessee River since the 1930s, was the model for the latter. Congress did not provide aid to education or create any new TVAs, but it did authorize many individual water projects as well as the construction of 800,000 units of low-cost public housing.

The history of public housing suggests some of the pitfalls of public investment. The postwar housing shortage created special problems for the poor, who often found themselves unable to afford rising rents. Many cities did retain price controls on rents after the war, but though such measures pleased apartment dwellers, they discouraged private construction of new rental units by making it hard for landlords to earn a profit. Thus controls intensified the existing shortage. Public housing advocates saw government-constructed and -managed housing as the remedy for the problem. Some also believed that the provision of good housing for the poor would solve other social problems—crime, prostitution, alcoholism—by creating a stable, comfortable environment for the disadvantaged. Unfortunately, over the long run, housing projects often became slums, dominated by the least stable elements among their tenants. Lawlessness proliferated, and physical conditions deteriorated quickly because of vandalism and poor maintenance. By the 1970s "the projects" were synonymous with poverty and crime.

Although it abandoned across-the-board price controls after the war, the Truman administration continued a variety of industry-specific regulations it had inherited. Most dated from the 1930s, though the origins of some stretched back to the turn of the century. Government bureaus like the Civil Aeronautics Board (CAB) and the Interstate Commerce Commission (ICC) determined what airlines, truckers, and railroads could haul, where, and at what price. In conjunction with state agencies, the Federal Power Commission (later renamed the Federal Energy Regulatory Commission) set prices for electricity, natural gas, and telephone service. The Securities and Exchange Commission (SEC) set rules for companies issuing securities and for stock market trading. Washington determined what sort of business financial institutions could transact, forcing firms to specialize in investment banking (securities), commercial banking (deposits and loans), mortgage lending, or insurance. It also imposed limits on both the interest commercial banks could offer savers and the commissions stockbrokers could charge investors, and state governments often imposed further restrictions on financial companies, for instance limiting the number of bank branches and imposing ceilings on interest rates charged borrowers. By the early 1950s industry-specific regulations covered about a quarter of the American economy.

Proponents of regulation like Truman argued that it corrected the errors of the marketplace. Utilities such as electricity, natural gas, and telephones enjoyed "natural monopolies." It was far cheaper for one company to supply everyone in a given area with power, telephones, or gas than for several firms to do so. These systems entailed huge fixed costs—expenses like stringing wire or laying pipe that accrued regardless of the level of sales—and firms could keep prices low only by spreading these expenses over as many consumers as possible. The government, however, needed to guarantee that such monopolies did not gouge consumers. In other cases, regulators believed that competition took destructive forms. Banks, for example, might seek higher returns by speculating with depositors' funds in securities markets, putting not only their own but also their customers' money at risk. In regulated sectors, regulations sought to impose "equitable" prices. Unfortunately this term is subjective, and in practice authorities focused on return on investment. They added up the total physical investment made by a firm, determined an admissible rate of return—usually 8 to 12 percent—and then set prices that would generate that level of profit. Often regulations sought social as well as economic ends. Washington allowed Savings & Loans to pay savers slightly higher interest rates than commercial banks but required them to funnel most of their money into home mortgages. Regulators allowed American Telephone and Telegraph (AT&T, or the Bell System), which enjoyed a national monopoly on telephone service, to charge high rates on long-distance calls to subsidize cheap local service. Truman did not expand this system, but he defended it energetically, most notably resisting attempts by natural gas producers (those who actually drilled for gas) to escape regulation.

The Truman administration also vigorously enforced the anti-trust laws. These measures, the oldest of which dated from the late nineteenth century, banned "restraint of trade" and various "unfair" competitive devices. Anti-trust advocates assumed that, left to themselves, businesses in the same industry would combine to form cartels or monopolies that would exploit consumers by raising prices and limiting output. These measures had broad impact. Firms that owned important patents had to share their knowledge. DuPont, the chemical firm that developed nylon, helped Monsanto establish itself in the nylon business chiefly to avoid anti-trust prosecution. Mergers between companies in the same field became nearly impossible unless one was near financial collapse. Unions between firms in related fields faced scrutiny as well. In the late 1950s, for instance, Washington prevented General Shoe, one of the country's largest makers of footwear, from purchasing retail outlets because, once purchased, these stores might favor the products of General Shoe over those of other shoemakers.

Whereas regulatory policy remained consistent throughout the Truman administration, the outbreak of the Korean War in 1950 forced major changes in other areas. After World War II the level of military spending declined sharply, hitting $13 billion in 1949, or less than 5 percent of GDP. This trend reversed sharply after 1950 as the war in Korea and the intensification of the cold war dictated a huge military buildup. By 1953 defense spending had increased to more than $52 billion, or 14 percent of GDP. Peace in Korea after 1953 allowed modest reductions, but military spending remained close to 10 percent of GDP for the rest of the decade.

In the short run, defense spending sparked an inflationary boom. The economy was already recovering from the 1949 recession when mobilization began, and the war in Korea created a buyers' panic. Consumers and businesses remembered the inflation associated with World War II and assumed that another war would bring comparable price increases. They bought in anticipation of inflation, creating shortages that drove prices up. By early 1951 consumer prices were increasing at an annual rate of 10 percent.

The administration responded aggressively. It persuaded Congress to raise taxes, returning rates to the high levels of World War II. In 1945 the basic income tax had stood at 23 percent, with rates increasing in several steps, culminating in a 94 percent rate on income above a certain (very high) level. In 1948 Congress had cut the basic rate to 16 percent and the top rate to 82 percent, with interim levies down proportionally. During the Korean War the basic rate returned to 22 and the top rate 92 percent, again with interim rates up proportionally. Taxes on corporations remained heavy as well, taking 40 to 50 percent of firms' net income. Although painful, these increases allowed the government to finance the war in Korea and its cold war buildup without a large deficit. The Truman administration also imposed wage-price controls, which largely ended panic buying. Finally, the government encouraged a substantial expansion of industrial capacity by offering generous tax concessions to companies that built new steel mills, aluminum smelters, and the like.

The Korean War also led to the rebirth of monetary policy, a change with far-reaching implications. The central bank, the Federal Reserve, issues currency and can to a large degree control interest rates. Early in World War II the Federal Reserve had agreed with the Treasury to "peg" interest rates at a very low level, 2.5 percent for long-term government bonds, and it expanded the money supply as needed to satisfy all borrowers at that rate. This policy had enabled the government to finance its staggering wartime borrowing cheaply, albeit by sharply expanding the supply of money. After 1945, however, the peg became

parties remained evenly balanced in Congress, and prosperity inclined the population as much against radical shifts of policy in a
conservative direction as in a liberal one. Moreover, many of the
programs inherited from Roosevelt and Truman had great support. As Eisenhower observed in a letter to one of his brothers,
"Should any political party attempt to abolish Social Security,
unemployment insurance, and eliminate labor laws and farm
programs, you would not hear from that party again in our political history."

In one area Truman and Eisenhower agreed: both sought balanced budgets. Like his predecessor, Eisenhower believed that
deficits fueled inflation, but he also saw the growth of federal
spending and borrowing as part of the government's tendency to
dominate the economy, which he deplored as "creeping socialism." But Eisenhower had a more difficult time than his predecessor constraining government outlays. Truman had been able
to cut defense spending to a fairly low level in the 1940s. In the
1950s the experience of the Korean War (which ended in 1953)
and the continuation of the cold war encouraged the maintenance of a powerful military. Pressure for defense outlays was
constant, and Eisenhower had to fight hard just to keep military
spending at 10 percent of GDP. Balancing budgets while spending heavily on the military worked against large tax cuts. The
only reduction of note in income taxes under Eisenhower came
after the end of the Korean War, when Congress cut the base rate
from 22 to 20 percent and the top rate from 92 to 90 percent, with
interim rates down accordingly. The president managed to balance only three of his eight budgets, but except for one year in
the wake of the 1957–1958 recession, the deficits were small. In
1960 total federal debt was $290 billion, or 55 percent of GDP,
down from 71 percent when Eisenhower took office.

Eisenhower reduced public investment substantially. He
abandoned plans inherited from the Truman administration to

increasingly controversial. With the economy prosperou
opportunities for profitable investment abounding, the der
for loans at 2.5 percent was extremely heavy. The Fed could
isfy this demand only by substantially expanding the suppl
money, an activity that, historically, had yielded inflation.

In the spring of 1951, after a long and divisive internal deb
the Treasury abandoned the peg. The sharp increase in pri
after the outbreak of the war in Korea, along with a surge in be
rowing and a substantial increase in the money supply, convinc
even many skeptics that the central bank could no longer provic
funds on demand at such a low rate. The new arrangement no
only allowed the Federal Reserve to raise interest rates but, in the
future, to set them at its own discretion. This effectively made
the central bank an autonomous center of economic policy. The
Treasury official who negotiated the new arrangement, William
McChesney Martin, Jr., soon became chairman of the board of
governors of the Federal Reserve System, the central bank's governing body, and by the end of the year the Federal Reserve had
allowed the interest rate on long-term U.S. government bonds to
rise to 3 percent. This, in combination with higher taxes and controls on wages and prices, was sufficient to bring inflation under
control.

CONSERVATIVE ECONOMICS

The accession of Republican Dwight D. Eisenhower to
the presidency in 1953 changed the emphasis of economic policy.
Truman's enthusiasm for public investment and government
regulation reflected grave doubts about the capacity of free enterprise to meet the country's social needs. In contrast, President
Eisenhower believed that in most cases—though not all—private enterprise could satisfy society's requirements. Like Truman, however, Eisenhower had limited room to maneuver. The

construct a huge, federally owned dam on the Snake River in the Northwest to generate power, instead allowing private firms to build several smaller dams. He refused to fund new TVA power plants with federal appropriations; rather he authorized the organization to raise money by selling bonds, putting the TVA on the same plane as private utilities. Public housing construction fell from ninety thousand units in 1951 to fewer than fifteen thousand in 1956. The administration dismantled the Reconstruction Finance Corporation, a depression-era bureau that made loans to private firms and local governments for various projects. The president did not automatically reject public investment—his support was critical to the creation of both the St. Lawrence Seaway, linking the Great Lakes with the Atlantic Ocean, and the interstate highway system. But these were not projects that anyone seriously expected private interests to fund.

Eisenhower also demonstrated less enthusiasm than Truman for regulation. Most notably, upon taking office he immediately terminated wage-price controls, even though the war in Korea was not yet over. Nevertheless prices remained stable, reinforcing the president's conviction that monetary and fiscal policy could effectively contain inflation without the need for direct controls. On regulations directed toward specific industries, Eisenhower proved less resolute. These measures often had public support, and the controlled businesses had usually learned to live with and even profit from regulation. Eisenhower's chairman of the Civil Aeronautics Board, which regulated airlines, did approve an unusually large number of new routes, guaranteeing that at least two airlines provided service between most major cities. The administration also initially backed efforts to remove natural gas production from regulation. But accusations that an oil company had tried to bribe a U.S. senator to secure his vote for reform led Eisenhower to revoke his support, wrecking the effort.

Initially Eisenhower's economic policies worked well. The end of the Korean War in 1953, which allowed a substantial drop in military spending, brought a mild recession in 1954, but the economy rebounded quickly, spurred by lower interest rates and a modest tax cut. The next two years were quite prosperous, with GDP increasing 9 percent and unemployment falling to 4 percent.

Eisenhower's second term was not as happy. In 1957 the economy fell into a deep recession that lasted eighteen months and saw unemployment surge past 7 percent, a postwar high. The recovery was strong but short-lived, and by the end of 1960 the economy was again shrinking. Occasional recessions are probably inevitable—perhaps even inherent to the capitalist system— but the 1957–1958 downturn was unusually deep, and the development of a new recession just two years later was unusual. Something more than the normal ebb and flow of economic life seems to have been at work.

The blame for this extended economic sluggishness quite likely resided with the government. By 1957 the Eisenhower administration had cut federal outlays to 16 percent of GDP, a level not seen again in the twentieth century. Unfortunately government did not match lower spending with lower taxes. It ran a $12 billion deficit in 1959, but that reflected the recession, which had cut tax revenue. In 1960 the government actually ran a small surplus despite an economic slowdown. The administration had created a situation in which Washington would take in much more than it spent, at least when the country was prosperous. This tended to dampen demand and slow the economy—critics referred to it as "fiscal drag." The Federal Reserve probably could have neutralized fiscal drag by reducing interest rates, in effect channeling Washington's surplus to the private sector. In fact, however, interest rates hit a postwar high in 1957, and after falling back somewhat during the recession, set another record in 1959.

Why did the administration and the Federal Reserve follow these policies? Critics, who included some Republicans as well as Democrats, warned that this program could create recession and urged tax cuts and lower interest rates. At the time many argued that Eisenhower and Fed chairman Martin had an irrational, ideological preference for balanced budgets and high interest rates that led them to follow inappropriate policies. This may have been the case, but a plausible economic rationale for their policies did exist. Prices increased by 3 percent both in 1957 and 1958, despite the recession. The country had certainly experienced inflation before, but in living memory it had been the product of war. Peacetime inflation, even at this relatively low level, was new and alarming. The administration and the Federal Reserve were determined to stabilize prices, and tight money and balanced budgets were the most obvious means to this end. Such policies would reduce the demand for goods and services, forcing sellers to hold prices in line. Just as alarming, in 1959 the United States experienced a deficit in its international balance of payments. Its trade surplus fell to less than $2 billion, a sum insufficient to finance foreign aid, military operations abroad, tourist travel, and private investment directed toward other countries. Dollars accumulated in the central banks of European countries, which began to redeem greenbacks in gold. Inflation reinforced this problem because, under the regime of fixed exchange rates, higher prices in the United States made American goods that much more expensive and less competitive abroad. Fiscal and monetary restraint would stabilize prices and cut the demand for foreign goods as well as for domestically produced ones, while high interest rates would attract the money of foreign investors to the United States.

Despite a measure of economic success, these policies created serious political problems for Eisenhower and the Republican party. Although painful, the 1957–1958 and 1960–1961 recessions were not disastrous. Between 1957 and 1961, production and employment both increased, though not as fast as in previous years. By the early 1960s inflation had stabilized below 2 percent, while the balance of payments had swung back into surplus. Eisenhower and Martin could reasonably argue that the country's long-term economic well-being demanded stable prices and a strong dollar. But the public refused to tolerate recession, whatever the reasons. The Democrats won large majorities in Congress in 1958, upsetting the approximate balance in the legislature that had lasted for twenty years. In 1960 Democrat John F. Kennedy defeated Richard Nixon, Eisenhower's vice president, to win the presidency in an extremely close election. In both campaigns the Democrats emphasized "hard times," which they blamed on the administration. The policies pursued by Eisenhower during his second term allowed people with very different ideas about the economy to take power.

2

The Go-Go Economy

IN THE 1960s the United States enjoyed greater prosperity than in any other decade of its history. Between 1960 and 1970 GDP increased 50 percent as income surged and unemployment fell. Good times bred exuberance, even hubris. Economists and government officials announced that they had conquered the business cycle. Companies expanded in every direction, confident that executives could manage a broad array of new responsibilities. Unfortunately hubris attracted nemesis. By 1970 the American economy was badly overextended, with many of the initiatives pursued by business and government turning out badly.

THE NEW ECONOMICS

Keynesian ideas dominated economic thinking in the 1960s, but these had evolved considerably from the Keynesianism of the 1940s. Prosperity had rendered obsolete those policies developed to deal with the Great Depression. Nevertheless economists still believed that Keynes had provided unique insights into economic life that, properly applied, offered useful prescriptions for the country's immediate problems. Proponents christened their approach the "New Economics."

Attention focused on the business cycle. Although the econ-

omy grew robustly in the 1940s and 1950s, it suffered from occasional recessions that halted expansion and left between one and
two million unemployed. These downturns entailed real and, in
the minds of reformers, avoidable hardships. The government,
Keynesians argued, could eliminate such swings by "fine tuning"
the demand for goods and services, a policy also known as "demand management." Armed with statistics on economic capacity
and projections of investment and consumer spending, Washington could manipulate its deficit to keep the demand for goods
and services at the optimal level, enough to provide full employment without stimulating inflation. The central bank would play
a secondary but significant role in this process, adjusting interest
rates as needed to make investment more or less attractive. As
Paul Samuelson, the country's leading Keynesian and the first
American recipient of the Nobel Prize in Economics, wrote,
"With proper fiscal and monetary policies, our economy can
have full employment and whatever rate of . . . growth it wants."

Keynesians also refined their thinking about inflation. Origi-
nally they saw inflation as the opposite of recession, with demand
in excess of supply pushing prices upward. This analysis
explained rising prices after World War II and during the Korean War fairly well. In 1957 and 1958, however, inflation accelerated even as the economy slipped into recession, suggesting
the need for a new approach. To explain this phenomenon,
Keynesian economists devised the Phillips Curve. The economist
A. W. Phillips, an Australian working in Britain, had observed
that, historically, inflation and unemployment had an inverse
relationship. If one was low, the other tended to be high. This relationship led Keynesians to postulate a trade-off between unemployment and inflation; improvement in one inevitably led to
deterioration in the other. They attributed this phenomenon to
economic "friction," the power of big business and large unions

to push prices and wages up in advance of demand and to keep them stable as sales and employment fell. Keynesians calculated that, as matters stood in the United States, 4 percent unemployment would entail 3 percent inflation, while inflation under 2 percent required unemployment of 5 to 6 percent. Forced to choose, most Keynesians would seek high employment rather than stable prices—the Great Depression and the mass unemployment that had accompanied it were their intellectual reference points. They did believe, however, that government policies restricting the "market power" of unions and big business could improve the trade-off between inflation and unemployment.

Many reformers sought not only greater prosperity but also different uses for the nation's wealth. They viewed the growth of personal consumption in the 1950s with disdain, seeing it, as journalist Theodore H. White wrote, "a torrent of self-indulgence . . . to the ultimate ruin of moral fiber and purpose." The nation should, reformers argued, devote more of its abundance to projects for the general good. The cold war reinforced this sentiment. Many reformers feared that the United States was falling behind the Soviet Union technologically and economically, an opinion reinforced in 1957 when the Soviets launched Sputnik, the first satellite to orbit the Earth. From the perspective of the twenty-first century, after the political and economic collapse of the Soviet Union, this concern seems ridiculous. But reformers' intellectual predilections often led them to overrate the Soviets. As advocates of public investment, they could not help but believe that the Soviet Union, which as a Communist state could mobilize huge resources for such activities, would outpace the United States unless Americans developed the same capability.

The New Economics in Practice

Upon taking office in January 1961, President Kennedy promised to "get the country moving again." Economic policy developed only gradually, however. Kennedy was not particularly knowledgeable about or interested in the subject, but he did staff the Council of Economic Advisers with such talented scholars as Walter Heller and James Tobin, who were committed to Keynesian ideas, and they eventually won over the president to their way of thinking. By the end of his second year in office, Kennedy had become an eloquent advocate of the New Economics.

Initially the administration focused on the recession it had inherited from the Eisenhower administration, which had forced unemployment to 6.7 percent. The CEA blamed the problem in part on "fiscal drag"—the tendency of the government to run a surplus even when the economy was well short of full employment. The CEA calculated that a $10 billion federal deficit would stimulate demand sufficiently to close this gap. But many in Congress opposed more spending, and economic recovery in the spring of 1961 robbed the matter of urgency.

At this point international crisis intervened. Several confrontations with the Soviet Union led Kennedy to expand military spending sharply. The military urged tax increases to finance this expense, but Kennedy, heeding advice from the CEA and no doubt realizing that taxes are never popular, decided instead to let the deficit rise. The government ran a deficit of $7 billion in fiscal 1962, up from $3 billion in 1961, despite a stronger economy.

The Federal Reserve contributed to expansion as well. It held interest rates stable even as the demand for loans increased, providing money to finance rising investment. With inflation low and the current account in surplus, such a liberal policy seemed reasonable. Politics played a part as well, however. Although an autonomous bureau, the Federal Reserve did not exist in a vacuum. The president appoints the members of the Federal Reserve Board, the central bank's governing body, and Congress, which created the Fed, can reorganize it. In practice the central bank cannot for long follow a policy sharply at odds with the executive branch. Kennedy and his advisers encouraged William Martin to keep rates stable and gave him reason to think that his reappointment as Fed chairman depended on compliance. This, as much as changing economic conditions, accounted for the shift of monetary policy between the Eisenhower and Kennedy administrations.

Meanwhile the CEA codified its goals, announcing that the administration would seek to drive unemployment down to 4 percent, which supposedly represented full employment. Full employment is a simple concept, connoting the point at which the number of people who want jobs equals the number of positions available. As an economist would say, it is the point at which the labor market "clears." Measuring it is another matter, however. Even at full employment, some people are between jobs and thus register as unemployed. As long as they find positions within a reasonable period, this does not constitute a serious social problem. The rate of unemployment that represents full employment therefore depends in part on the structure of labor markets, which can change. In 1962 the CEA's 4 percent estimate reflected a consensus among economists and was probably realistic. Over time, however, this number became sacrosanct, guiding policy even though conditions had changed.

The administration did not ignore inflation or the balance of payments. Although inflation was low and the current account in surplus, deterioration of either might force the government to abandon fiscal and monetary stimulus. The Phillips Curve suggested that, as unemployment fell to 4 percent, inflation would rise to 3 percent, a level many considered unacceptable. To forestall this, in early 1962 the CEA announced "guidelines" for wages and prices. It reasoned that because productivity was increasing at 3 percent a year, wages could increase that fast without driving prices higher. Accordingly, the guidelines declared that wages should rise 3 percent a year while prices ought to remain stable.

Although the guidelines had no basis in law, business soon learned not to ignore them. In early 1962 the administration persuaded the steelworkers' union to accept raises of only 3 percent. Later the largest steel producers, led by U.S. Steel, announced price increases of 6 percent. Kennedy publicly denounced the increase and brought all his power to bear on the industry. He steered government orders to the few steel firms that held prices down and, more questionably, had federal agents harass steel executives. The industry eventually abandoned the higher prices, and the CEA guidelines became standard for large firms and unions.

Efforts to protect the balance of payments also relied on direct action. Although in the early and mid-1960s the United States ran large surpluses on its current account, substantial sums flowed out of the country to finance aid, military operations abroad, and foreign investment, creating a deficit on the capital account that consumed this surplus. To limit outflows, the Kennedy administration persuaded Congress to impose an "interest equalization tax," which made the purchase of foreign securities by Americans prohibitively expensive. Some could evade the tax. In particular, large American firms could finance new operations abroad themselves, simply by transferring money from one corporate division to another. Using such methods, companies like Ford, General Electric, and Procter & Gamble continued to expand their presence in Europe throughout the

1960s. Foreign borrowers, however, found that the tax made it very difficult to raise money in the United States.

The interest equalization tax had long-term negative consequences. Foreign borrowers did not disappear but went to London rather than New York. There a growing cadre of investment bankers underwrote securities for these borrowers denominated in dollars that they then sold to the substantial number of foreigners who, by the early 1960s, held greenbacks outside the United States. The Eurobond or Eurodollar market, as it became known, grew fast in the 1960s and 1970s, allowing London to reclaim, at least in part, the role as center of international finance that it had lost to New York during World War I.

In early 1963 President Kennedy proposed a bold initiative that effectively announced his conversion to the New Economics. He suggested a tax cut even though the economy was prosperous. Kennedy argued that the economy could grow faster still, pointing to an unemployment rate that stubbornly failed to decline below 5 percent. He also claimed that more rapid economic expansion would pay for at least part of the tax reduction. His proposal would reduce the basic tax on income from 20 to 14 percent and the top rate from 90 to 70 percent, with other rates down proportionally. Corporate levies would decline too. Resistance came from some conservatives who objected to deficit financing, and from some liberals like John Kenneth Galbraith who argued that the government should spend more on social services rather than cut taxes and who described Kennedy's plan as "reactionary Keynesianism." The measure did, however, enjoy the support of business groups whose members stood to benefit from lower taxes. The tax cut became law in 1964, after Kennedy's death.

The New Economics yielded favorable results through 1965. Over five years, inflation registered less than 2 percent a year, a level so low that many economists considered it synonymous with price stability. Production expanded by 27 percent over these years, and joblessness fell from 6.7 to 4.5 percent. The federal government did run a modest deficit each year, but rapid economic growth meant that total federal debt as a percentage of GDP fell from 55 percent to 44 percent. Meanwhile the current account showed a surplus of more than $6 billion in 1964 and $5 billion in 1965, the highest levels since the immediate postwar era. These accomplishments owed something to Eisenhower's success in curbing inflation, but the Kennedy administration had made the most of its opportunities.

Kennedy's successor, Lyndon B. Johnson, undertook an ambitious program of public investment. Franklin D. Roosevelt was his hero, and, like FDR, Johnson attacked social problems with federal legislation and money. This effort, which Johnson christened the Great Society, had near-utopian aims. According to the president, "It demands an end to poverty and racial injustice—to which we are totally committed in our time, but that is just the beginning. The Great Society is a place where every child can find knowledge to enrich his mind and enlarge his talents. It is a place where leisure is a welcome chance to build and reflect. . . . It is a place where the city of man serves not only the needs of the body and the demands of commerce, but the desire for beauty and the hunger for community. It is a place where man can renew contact with nature." As the president said in 1964, "We're in favor of a lot of things, and we're against mighty few." The government appropriated more money for public housing and urban renewal, made contributions to local school budgets, funded public television and the National Endowments for the Arts and the Humanities, and provided benefits for the poor such as preschool education and food stamps. Some of these government investments were relatively modest, but others were quite expensive. Federal spending on domestic programs increased from 7.1 percent of GDP in 1960 to 9.4 percent of GDP in 1968, an increase of about one-third.

The Great Society had perhaps its greatest economic impact through the reform of health care. In 1965 Congress created Medicare (health insurance for the elderly) and Medicaid (health insurance for the poor). These measures freed millions from the threat of ruinous medical bills or, even worse, denial of care because they could not pay. Generous federal compensation also encouraged the development of new treatments that might otherwise not have become available as rapidly. But Medicare and Medicaid were "cost-plus" programs: in effect, they allowed doctors and hospitals to set reimbursement. Lacking incentives to do so, patients and doctors paid little attention to costs, and expenses quickly spiraled out of control. In 1968, 5 percent of federal spending went to health-care programs; by 1980 the figure was 9.4 percent; and by 2000 Medicare and Medicaid absorbed almost 20 percent of Washington's outlays. The federal government had lost control of a growing part of its budget, and because Washington's payment schedule set the pace for the entire health-care industry, overall expenses in the sector grew faster than they probably would have otherwise.

THE GO-GO STOCK MARKET

Even as President Johnson pushed one Great Society program after another through Congress, the greatest stock market boom in the country's history to that point approached culmination. During the 1930s terrible losses on stocks as well as some widely publicized scandals had soured an entire generation on common stocks (equities). But during the 1950s the situation changed. Higher incomes gave people more money to invest, even as inflation made it hard for savers using conservative investments like savings accounts, which paid as little as 1 percent, to keep up with rising prices. Meanwhile the stock of well-established companies like General Motors and Standard Oil (Exxon) earned annual dividends of 7 percent. The tax code further encouraged investment in stocks. The government taxed capital gains at a far lower rate than income, so investments like equities that could yield capital gains were more attractive than those that simply paid interest.

Stockbrokers encouraged this trend, with Merrill Lynch leading the way. The events of the 1930s had given brokers a bad reputation and convinced much of the public that financial markets were a sort of sophisticated casino. Merrill sought to change this. It carefully trained its brokers, providing them with solid research on investment prospects and emphasizing the importance of recommending investments appropriate to clients' individual needs. Most dramatically, it put its brokers on salary, abolishing the traditional practice of paying them a portion of the commissions they generated. Merrill also advertised aggressively, running newspaper and magazine copy with titles like, "What Everybody Ought to Know About This Stock and Bond Business." The idea was to convince people with money that equities represented a safe and lucrative long-term investment. Other firms copied Merrill's approach, though none was quite as successful. The exchanges advertised as well, with the New York Stock Exchange (NYSE) touting stock ownership as the route to "People's Capitalism."

Money poured into financial markets. Trading on the New York Stock Exchange expanded from as few as 500,000 shares a day in the mid-1940s to 12 million shares a day in 1968. The Dow Jones industrial average, an index of the prices of leading equities, rose from 200 in 1950 to 1000 in 1966. The number of Americans owning stocks went from 6.5 million in 1952 to 32 million in 1970. Five million Americans had mutual fund accounts in

1960; ten million owned them in 1969. Pension funds and insurance companies, which had traditionally invested in bonds and real estate, began to buy stocks.

The growth of financial markets had broad implications. An established, respected company could raise money on very good terms by selling its shares to the public. IBM and the Aluminum Company of America (Alcoa), for instance, financed their rapid expansion by selling stock. Entrepreneurial ventures that might not qualify for bank loans could place securities with investors who were willing to take a risk for the chance of high returns. Finally, middle-class investors, if they bought wisely, could secure for themselves more of the benefits of the country's rapid economic growth.

The stock market boom of the 1960s also encouraged one of the greatest waves of mergers in American history. Two thousand firms disappeared through merger in 1965, and the number climbed to 6,500 in 1969. This blistering pace largely reflected the activities of conglomerates, firms composed of many otherwise unrelated divisions.

Conglomerates stood at the intersection of several economic trends. The United States has always had empire builders who constructed huge firms by merging smaller ones. Before 1930, however, these combinations usually involved firms in related fields. William C. Durant, for instance, assembled General Motors out of dozens of firms making automobiles or automobile parts. But stricter enforcement of anti-trust laws after 1945 put an end to such mergers, forcing would-be empire builders to construct their domains from unrelated firms. Management theory encouraged this development. In the 1950s and 1960s managers increasingly argued that their skills were universal; the qualities required to run a textile mill would also work for a chain of restaurants. Sophisticated financial controls and a multi-divisional structure would allow managers to track the performance of and guide a number of otherwise unrelated businesses. Conglomerates would identify the most promising industries and buy companies operating there, securing high profits and rapid growth. A diverse collection of businesses would also insulate a company against serious declines in any one industry. These ideas were particularly appealing because many firms that had expanded rapidly over the preceding twenty years were finding it difficult to maintain growth as their markets became saturated and, in some cases, as foreign competition became tougher.

The booming stock market provided another impetus for the growth of conglomerates. In the 1950s and 1960s the equities of companies with a reputation for rapid growth in earnings commanded high prices. Conglomerates usually enjoyed such reputations, and so their equities sold at a premium. Stock became the currency with which they acquired other firms—they exchanged their own shares for those of merger partners. Conglomerates could afford this because, contrary to the popular image, their targets were often profitable but slow-growing firms with low stock prices. The earnings of acquired companies then enhanced the per share profits of the conglomerate, pushing the stock price even higher and allowing further acquisitions.

By the late 1960s, firms like International Telephone and Telegraph (ITT), Gulf & Western, Textron, Ling-Temco-Vought (LTV), and a few dozen smaller conglomerates controlled hundreds of unrelated businesses. Textron sold zippers, pens, snowmobiles, eyeglass frames, silverware, golf carts, machine tools, helicopters, rocket engines, ball bearings, and gas meters. The largest conglomerate, ITT, had 150 separate divisions or profit centers. Even firms not generally considered conglomerates sought to grow by diversifying into unrelated fields. RCA dominated a dynamic industry, producing consumer electronics and managing the National Broadcasting Corporation (NBC), but it expanded by purchasing companies that printed books, made carpets and frozen food, and leased automobiles, even while building its own line of computers in a futile attempt to challenge IBM.

The vogue for conglomerates ended badly. To succeed over the long run, a conglomerate had to improve the management of the firms it purchased. In some cases this happened; Gulf & Western substantially upgraded the operations of Paramount Pictures after acquiring it. But in many instances the firms acquired were already well managed, leaving little room for improvement. Moreover, as conglomerates grew, their central offices were less and less able to oversee effectively the affairs of various divisions. In 1970 the stock prices of conglomerates collapsed after many of them reported lower earnings. These firms struggled throughout the next decade as most sold off divisions almost as fast as they had bought them in the 1960s. Most of these firms then focused their attention on one or two lines of business. Gulf & Western became Paramount, a leading media company; LTV concentrated, far less successfully, on making steel.

The conglomerate episode had far-ranging consequences. For a decade the managers of many of the country's leading firms concentrated on making deals rather than on improving operations. And these deals did not reinforce firms' central businesses but spread managers' attention ever thinner. Although impossible to quantify, such distractions must have substantially hurt the performance of American industry. There is little doubt that in some cases, like RCA, the mania for diversification contributed to firms' long-term decline.

The conglomerate craze also spawned an important structural change in the economy. Whereas earlier waves of mergers at the turn of the century and in the 1920s had proceeded in an ad hoc manner, that of the 1960s created an institutional infrastructure that, in effect, made the process permanent. Investment banks like Morgan Stanley created profitable mergers and acquisition departments (M&A) which long outlasted the fashion for conglomerates, constituting a permanent market for companies and the divisions of companies.

THE SERVICE ECONOMY

The growth of financial services constituted part of a broader expansion of service industries throughout the postwar era. In 1945 manufacturing employed 15 million; services, excluding government, 19 million. By 1970, 19 million people worked in factories, 32 million in services. During the 1970s the trend accelerated, with the number of manufacturing workers barely changing at all even as those in services increased 50 percent.

The growth of services reflected several factors. As incomes increased, Americans increasingly spent their money on products once considered luxuries, such as vacations and restaurant meals. For much of the middle class, shopping became an enjoyable pastime as much as a search for goods. In retailing alone the number of workers increased from 7 million in 1945 to 15 million in 1970. Higher education grew dramatically as the middle class sent more of its children to college and white-collar jobs increasingly required a college degree—22 million Americans had college degrees in 1970 compared with 9 million twenty years earlier. In other instances, changes within an industry sparked growth. New discoveries in medicine allowed doctors to treat ailments once incurable, and the development of health insurance, both government and private, made the best care available to more people. Spending on health care in 1940 totaled less than $4 billion; in 1970 it totaled $71 billion, a 924 percent increase in real (inflation-adjusted) terms. Even many of the new industries that centered on manufacturing included a large service component.

Television required broadcasting stations and programming; computers created a demand for data processing.

American entrepreneurs eagerly seized on the opportunities available in services. With the important exceptions of transportation, utilities, and telecommunications, services had traditionally been the province of small business. Restaurants, hotels, barbershops, and dry cleaners were overwhelmingly owner-operated. Even in retailing, national chains like Sears, Walgreen's, and A&P had to compete with locally owned department stores, pharmacies, and grocery stores. Hospitals were generally stand-alone organizations run by churches, foundations, universities, or groups of local doctors. These fields were open for ambitious businessmen to organize, if they could.

Restaurants provided the model for much of this growth. In 1954 Ray Kroc purchased the right to franchise McDonald's, a California drive-in. The McDonald brothers had made their restaurant a success by stressing low prices and high turnover, an approach that required high productivity. Each employee had one clearly defined responsibility, like fry cook, and the restaurant used machinery designed for specific purposes, like making milkshakes. Essentially McDonald's applied to restaurants the devices of mass production pioneered by American manufacturers and retailers. Kroc and his associates took this model and expanded it rapidly through a network of franchises. The technique was not new, but the way McDonald's used it was. Traditionally a franchisee in a service industry purchased limited rights to a trademark or a technology with a one-time payment. After that, success or failure was his or her responsibility. McDonald's, however, forged a permanent relationship with its franchisees, claiming a fixed percentage of their gross revenues, providing ongoing support with advertising and new products, and strictly regulating the operations of their restaurants in order to maintain quality. McDonald's was also able to secure economies of scale by advertising and purchasing in bulk for the restaurants associated with it. By the 1980s, for example, it was the world's largest buyer of potatoes. For their part, franchisees brought capital and, far more important, energy and devotion. McDonald's represented a symbiotic fusion between big and small business.

Other entrepreneurs copied these tactics, often with almost as much success as Kroc. In the lodging industry, Holiday Inn led the way; in automotive repair and service, Midas Muffler and Mr. Transmission enjoyed considerable success; so did Orkin and Terminix in pest control. Successful chains offered a product that was good and, perhaps just as important, consistent. A customer who entered a McDonald's or Holiday Inn knew exactly what to expect, wherever the location.

In some cases small businesses themselves created mechanisms for coordination. They banded together in cooperatives that purchased in bulk and advertised for members, securing for themselves the considerable economies of scale available in these areas. The Independent Grocers Association (IGA) had limited success in helping members compete with grocery chains like Safeway and Kroger's, but the Ace and True Value cooperatives, which consisted of hardware stores, proved a boon to members, whose industry remained the province of owner-operators into the twenty-first century.

In services as in manufacturing, some firms grew by catering to the government. When Ross Perot, a former IBM salesman, founded Electronic Data Systems (EDS) in the early 1960s to provide data processing for private organizations, his first clients were hospitals in need of help with the complex billing requirements of Medicare and Medicaid. When Humana and Hospital Corporation of America (HCA) organized in the 1960s to purchase and manage hospitals, they not only imposed sophisticated management practices on their properties but also centralized and computerized Medicare and Medicaid billing. Their rapid expansion and high profits owed much to generous government compensation under these programs.

THE NEW ECONOMICS IN TROUBLE

In the late 1960s the New Economics lost ground. In part the problem reflected political miscalculations, but intellectual failings played a role as well. The New Economics assumed that economic performance depended on government spending, taxes, and borrowing, which authorities could adjust to keep demand at the optimal level. This, in turn, assumed that politicians would give economic concerns priority. Between 1961 and 1965, economists' desire for stimulus coincided with politicians' desire to cut taxes and increase military and social spending. After 1965, however, political and economic factors pulled in different directions.

The Vietnam War constituted the chief problem. In 1965 the economy was at a happy equilibrium, with full employment and stable prices. Johnson's Council of Economic Advisers argued that Washington needed to avoid any dramatic shift in spending and taxes that would upset this balance. Unfortunately it did not take into account the cost of the rapidly escalating war in Vietnam. Between fiscal 1965 and fiscal 1968, when the military effort there peaked, defense outlays increased 60 percent. This extra spending fell on an economy already operating near capacity and so translated into higher prices. In 1966, consumer prices increased by almost 3 percent, the largest jump in eight years. Inflation quickly wrecked the wage-price guidelines. Unions were unwilling to settle for 3 percent raises when prices were going up just as fast, and employers, enjoying robust demand for their products, granted increases knowing that they could pass rising costs on to consumers.

First and foremost, inflation reflected political calculations—
or miscalculations. In part the government simply underestimated the expense of the war in Vietnam, where at first the
administration hoped for a quick victory. But as the war continued and victory proved elusive, President Johnson intentionally
understated the war's expense by a large margin both to Congress and to his own economists. He realized that many, including the CEA and the military, would argue that the government
could not afford both the Vietnam War and the Great Society
without tax increases. But Johnson also anticipated that, confronted with these options, conservatives in Congress would demand cuts in Great Society outlays while liberals there might
well turn against the war. Facing these possibilities, Johnson decided to ignore the problem.

Almost by default, the Federal Reserve took the lead in resisting inflation. In the summer of 1966 it raised interest rates
sharply, with the prime rate—the rate banks charged their
largest and most creditworthy customers—hitting 6.5 percent, a
postwar record. In some areas, such as home mortgages, money
became unattainable at any price, and in 1967 economic growth
slowed dramatically. Ideally, slower growth would force companies to hold prices in line. At this point, however, fearing that it
had overreacted, and under intense pressure from the White
House to reverse course, the Fed cut interest rates.

In retrospect the central bank reversed itself too quickly. The
federal government probably could have fought the Vietnam
War and financed the Great Society without tax increases or
much inflation had the central bank raised interest rates and
kept them up. This policy would, in effect, have counterbalanced
higher government spending by choking off private investment.
Here, intellectual errors intervened. First, the CEA and many at
the Fed underestimated the strength of inflation, calculating that
the brief slowdown in 1967 was sufficient to halt it. The entire

Keynesian intellectual tradition focused on unemployment, and the Phillips Curve, by postulating that low unemployment might inevitably entail rising prices, led economists to tolerate inflation as the lesser of two evils. As a result, the dangers of inflation received short shrift. Second, Keynesians underestimated the ability of the Fed to affect economic performance. They considered federal spending and taxes the essence of economic policy and doubted that the central bank could maintain stability in the face of inappropriate fiscal policy. Nor did it help that President Johnson instinctively recoiled from higher interest rates, believing them as unpopular as higher taxes. In this he was almost certainly wrong. The political cost of high interest rates, while not negligible, was probably not as great as that of tax increases or inflation.

An international crisis in 1968 finally forced action. Because of lower interest rates and heavy military spending, the economy quickly rebounded from the 1967 slowdown. Low unemployment and strong demand led, in turn, to higher prices. In 1968 inflation stood at more than 4 percent, the highest level since the Korean War. In general, strong demand attracted imports, and under the system of fixed exchange rates, inflation made U.S. goods that much less competitive in international markets. These factors cut sharply into the current account surplus, which in 1968 totaled only $600 million. When the money sent abroad by Americans as aid, to pay for the war in Vietnam, and to finance investments (the capital account) was taken into account, dollars were flowing out of the country in huge quantities.

Pressures appeared on two fronts. Other industrial countries, which pegged their currencies to the dollar, had to buy all greenbacks offered at a fixed rate to maintain their pegs. Therefore, as dollars flowed abroad they gravitated to the central banks of Europe and Japan. Washington had agreed to redeem dollars held by other governments in gold at $35 an ounce, but by 1968 other

countries' dollar holdings far exceeded Washington's gold reserves. A sudden rush by other countries to turn dollars into the
precious metal could exhaust U.S. gold reserves. Developments
in the private gold market constituted a more immediate problem, however. Although American law banned private ownership of the precious metal, such was not the case elsewhere. Gold
traded actively in London, where Europe's central banks bought
it from and sold it to private brokers as necessary to maintain the
official price of $35 an ounce. Concerns about the American bal-
ance of payments, however, led to a flood of gold-buying in 1968
that threatened to exhaust European gold reserves and increased
the pressure on the continent's central banks to convert their dollars into gold.

Fearing a financial panic, the Johnson administration finally
acted. The president persuaded Congress to impose a surcharge
on income taxes, requiring all filers to pay 10 percent more than
they would otherwise—the war tax Johnson had sought to avoid.
The government also held outlays in line. Spending for fiscal
1969, which started in July 1968, increased only 3.1 percent over
the previous year, less than the increase in prices. The administration further strengthened the interest equalization tax to keep
dollars from leaving the country. Meanwhile the Federal Reserve
allowed interest rates to creep back near their 1966 highs. These
measures, the administration hoped, would halt inflation and
improve the balance of payments.

To deal with the immediate crisis in the gold market, the
United States reached an unusual agreement with the other industrial democracies. They all withdrew from the private gold
market, allowing the price there to rise above $35 an ounce.
Meanwhile governments promised to continue to exchange gold
at $35 an ounce among themselves, but not to buy from or sell to
outsiders. The result was a "two-tiered" market in which gov-

ernments essentially ignored private trading in the precious metal.

Beneath this legal fiction lay some unpleasant realities. It was clear that the United States had no intention of honoring its commitment to redeem dollars held by other countries in gold at $35 an ounce. Since the dollar was the foundation of international finance, this raised questions about the stability of the whole system. If the dollar was no longer "as good as gold," what exactly were it and the world's other currencies worth? It did not seem likely that the American balance of payments would improve enough to restore faith in the greenback. Most currency pegs dated from the late 1940s, when the economies of Europe and Japan had been struggling to recover from the war. By the late 1960s these economies had achieved a strength unimaginable twenty years earlier. In particular, their manufacturing productivity had grown faster than in the United States, making their exports more competitive. To expand its payments surplus substantially, the United States would probably have to devalue the dollar against the other major currencies, particularly the Japanese yen and the German deutschemark. This would make U.S. exports cheaper and its imports more expensive, encouraging the former and discouraging the latter. Unfortunately the Bretton Woods system made it very difficult to devalue the dollar because the greenback had no peg to change. The United States could raise the official price of gold, which would have the effect of devaluation, but many opposed this because it would reward those who had bought gold in international markets, undermining the dollar in the first place. A simultaneous revaluation of all the world's other currencies, increasing their pegs, would have the same result as devaluation, but such a measure entailed immense administrative and political complications because it required so many countries to act in concert. A protracted period of fiscal and monetary restraint, such as that imposed by Eisenhower and the Fed in the late 1950s, might resolve the problem by forcing U.S. prices down. But most officials believed such a policy would be politically disastrous. It had seriously hurt the popularity of Eisenhower and the Republican party in the late 1950s, and assertions throughout the 1960s by government officials and economists that recessions were avoidable had made the public even less tolerant of economic hardship. Overall the Johnson administration seemed content to drift, hoping that somehow these problems would resolve themselves.

The Monetarist Challenge

In the late 1960s monetarist economists challenged what had by then become Keynesian orthodoxy. They argued that, in the short run, the supply of money had more influence on economic performance than any other factor. If the supply of money grew too fast, people used the cash to bid prices up, creating inflation; if too little money was available, people lacked the cash to buy, creating recession. The leading monetarist economist was Milton Friedman, whose *Monetary History of the United States* (written with Anna Schwartz) demonstrated a strong, though hardly perfect, correlation between economic performance and changes in the money supply. Most notably, Friedman showed that the supply of money had contracted by one-third between 1929 and 1933, explaining the Great Depression.

The power of money had limits, however. Over the long run, economic growth depended on "real" factors like investment, the supply of raw materials, technology, the skills of the workforce, and so on. Monetary policy could not affect these.

Monetarism entailed a very different philosophy of government from Keynesian economics. Whereas most Keynesians believed that only government intervention could keep the economy stable, monetarists generally saw the private economy as naturally stable and attributed most problems to government mismanagement of the money supply. Whereas Keynesians emphasized fiscal policy—taxes, spending, and government borrowing—monetarists saw the Federal Reserve, which controlled the supply of money and interest rates, as the chief instrument of economic policy. Whereas Keynesians sought to "fine tune" the economy, monetarists argued that government policy should follow a consistent rule, expanding the money supply at a constant rate that was high enough to allow steady growth but not so high as to fuel inflation.

Keynesian economists strongly resisted monetarist arguments, focusing on an apparently technical point with great practical importance: the rate at which people spent money. Monetarists assumed that this figure, known as "velocity," was stable. Keynesians denied this, arguing that the propensity of individuals and firms to spend changed with conditions. If optimistic, they spent money readily; if pessimistic, they hoarded cash. An unstable velocity meant that changes in the money supply would not correlate with economic performance.

Monetarist thinking gained acceptance throughout the late 1960s and early 1970s, when changes in the money supply did roughly parallel economic performance. The strong reaction of the economy to changes in Fed policy in 1966 and 1967—slowing down and then speeding up as interest rates rose sharply and then fell—provided a convincing demonstration of the power of monetary policy. Practical considerations had influence as well. Monetary policy is easier to manage than fiscal policy. Both houses of Congress must approve any change in spending and taxes, and measures may take months to become law. Kennedy's tax cut, for instance, went into effect eighteen months after he proposed it. The Fed, in contrast, can change monetary policy almost instantly. This fact inclined even many Keynesians to place more emphasis on monetary policy. And monetarism seemed to address the country's immediate problems better than Keynes's ideas. Keynes had written in response to the depression, which by the late 1960s was a generation in the past. Monetarism spoke to the issue of inflation, a more immediate concern. Milton Friedman's observation that "inflation is always and everywhere a monetary phenomenon" promised a simple, straightforward answer to rising prices, just as Keynes's program of deficit spending had done for the depression.

Milton Friedman also reappraised the Phillips Curve. Most Keynesian economists assumed an inverse relationship between inflation and unemployment that required society to accept certain trade-offs. Friedman, in contrast, posited a "natural rate of unemployment," a level of joblessness consistent with stable prices and determined by the labor market. A country could reduce unemployment below this rate only by somehow reducing the cost of labor, which would allow firms to increase hiring. Inflation did this by effectively reducing the value of money in which wages were paid. But any gain in employment from inflation was only temporary. Workers would notice that their wages were not keeping up with prices and would demand raises, increasing labor costs and returning employment to its old level. Further doses of inflation might delay adjustment, but eventually workers would start adding anticipated inflation into their wage demands. The resulting spiral of rising wages and prices would institutionalize inflation without reducing long-term unemployment. According to Friedman's analysis, the Phillips Curve was not only wrong but dangerous, a statistical mirage that lured countries into a poor bargain. In exchange for a temporary drop in unemployment, they got a permanent increase in inflation. In time, Friedman's thinking on this subject would enjoy wide acceptance, even among Keynesians.

Nixon's Economy

Upon becoming president in January 1969, Richard Nixon inherited a variety of problems. The country was fighting a costly and apparently unwinnable war in Vietnam; unrest in the nation's universities and ghettos seemed to threaten social order; and much of Lyndon Johnson's Great Society remained unfinished. Inflation was approaching an annual rate of 6 percent, the highest level since the Korean War, and the imbalance of international payments remained large. Nixon's political weakness compounded these difficulties. The Democrats had solid majorities in both houses of Congress and were not inclined to cooperate with the president, who for most of his career had been a fierce Republican partisan.

Nixon approached economic policy in a pragmatic—even opportunistic—fashion. As a Republican and a conservative, he instinctively favored free markets and sought to reduce government spending, taxes, and borrowing. Nixon also employed several eminent economists, most notably Arthur Burns and George Shultz, who knew Milton Friedman and accepted many, though not all, of his ideas. But Nixon's chief interests were politics and foreign affairs, not economics. Moreover, he attributed his loss of the extremely close 1960 presidential election to the recession of that year, which he blamed on Eisenhower's economic policies. Nixon was determined never again to risk his political career for economic principle.

Initially Nixon and his advisers concentrated on inflation, which they believed the government could tame relatively easily. Their plans drew heavily on Friedman's thinking about the natural rate of unemployment. Nixon's CEA, taking its cue from the Kennedy administration, assumed that 4 percent represented the natural rate of unemployment—that is, the level the country could maintain without accelerating inflation. The CEA further calculated that if joblessness increased slightly above this level, to a still-low 4.5 percent, the pressure of idle workers and unused capacity would slow increases in wages and prices. This gradual approach to stabilizing prices would take time, perhaps as much as two years, but it would avoid recession and the concomitant human and political damage. To this end the Nixon administration used fiscal and monetary restraint to slow the economy. It balanced the budget for fiscal 1969, cutting spending below Johnson's already cautious outlays, and it persuaded Congress to continue Johnson's income tax surcharge through fiscal 1970, albeit at 5 rather than 10 percent. Meanwhile the Federal Reserve increased interest rates sharply; they hit another postwar record at the end of 1969, with the prime rate peaking at 8.5 percent.

The results were disappointing. In 1970 the economy slid into recession, with unemployment increasing from 3.5 to 6 percent, the highest level in a decade. Although not severe by historical standards, the downturn worried the president, who associated recession with political defeat. Perhaps worse, price increases remained high, above 5 percent annually. Despite stubborn inflation, the government responded to the recession. The Fed cut interest rates, with the prime rate going from 8.5 percent in 1969 to less than 6 percent in 1971, and Washington ran a deficit of more than $20 billion in 1971. But inflation limited the amount of economic stimulus the federal government could safely provide, because more spending and lower interest rates might well translate into higher prices rather than greater output. The president's critics coined the term "stagflation" to describe the situation and urged more stimulus as well as direct intervention along the lines of Kennedy's wage-price guidelines to contain prices.

In retrospect the country was fortunate that conditions were not worse. Prosperity covers many errors, and a decade of good times had allowed problems in many sectors to multiply and fester. In the late 1960s speculative buying had sent the stock market to unsustainable levels, as money poured into the equities of firms with exaggerated or, in some cases, nonexistent prospects. The recession cut sharply into earnings and brought investors back to reality. In 1970 the Dow Jones industrial index declined 15 percent, from a little under 1000 to a little over 800, and speculative issues fell more. The decline in the stock market led to a sharp drop in trading and imposed punishing losses on brokers. In 1970 more than 100 firms that did business on the New York Stock Exchange disappeared—liquidated or merged with stronger firms. The federal government helped sort out the mess, creating an insurance fund for brokerage customers so that they need not fear losing money in the collapse of a firm with which they had an account.

Problems extended well beyond Wall Street. In June 1970 the Penn Central Railroad, the nation's largest, declared bankruptcy. Competition from automobiles, trucks, and airlines had hurt the company, as had bad management that, among other things, had involved the firm deeply in Florida real estate. Although railroads were not as important as they once were, the Penn Central remained vital to transportation in the Northeast and Midwest, and default on its gigantic debts threatened to drag many of its creditors into bankruptcy. Ultimately Washington, despairing of any other solution, nationalized the Penn Central, renaming it Conrail and launching an expensive effort to rehabilitate it. The government also created Amtrak, which took over passenger rail service throughout the country. Private railroads happily gave Washington their passenger operations, which had been losing money for years. In 1971 the federal government also extended loan guarantees to rescue the aerospace company Lockheed, which had overextended itself in developing the L-1011 "jumbo jet." Fortunately Lockheed resolved its difficulties short of bankruptcy.

From the perspective of the broader economy, escalating wages were the chief problem. In 1971 a modest recovery began and inflation fell somewhat, to a rate of about 4 percent, but a series of contracts negotiated by organized labor seemed to threaten progress. These agreements provided for raises averaging 8.4 percent a year over three years. Even with solid gains in productivity, these contracts apparently guaranteed price increases of 5 percent a year across a broad range of industries. Changes in the labor market, particularly the greater mobility of workers, meant that by 1970 full employment probably no longer meant 4 percent unemployment but rather 5 or 5.5 percent. Accordingly, the level of joblessness in 1971—5.5 percent—posed little threat to workers and so exercised few restraints on wage demands. Moreover, years of rising prices had led companies to assume that they could pass higher wages along to consumers in the form of higher prices, limiting their resistance to union demands. Some form of guidelines or controls seemed the easiest way to resolve the problem. Arthur Burns, whom Nixon had placed in charge of the Federal Reserve upon William McChesney Martin's retirement in 1970, urged just that on the president. Meanwhile Democrats in Congress gave the president legal authority to impose controls on wages and prices, believing that Nixon, who had often expressed strong dislike for controls, would never actually do so. They cynically hoped the existence of such power would embarrass the president. In cynicism, however, Nixon would prove more than their equal.

As had been the case with Johnson in 1968, an international crisis forced Nixon to act. During 1969 and 1970 the position of the dollar in international markets had strengthened. High interest rates had attracted money to the United States, and the recession had cut the demand for imported goods. But economic recovery in 1971 and falling interest rates quickly undid this progress. That year the United States ran its first current account deficit in a decade. Even more alarming, the trade balance swung into deficit for the first time in the twentieth century, with the country buying more abroad than it sold. Holders of greenbacks sold, and dollars piled up in the central banks of Europe and Japan, which were obligated under the Bretton Woods agreements to buy all dollars offered at the stated pegs. Other countries began to worry about the long-term value of their growing stock of greenbacks, as well as about the impact on their economies of issuing new currency to buy all these dollars. In August the Bank of England asked Washington to guarantee the $3 billion it held against devaluation, but the communiqué somehow became garbled, and the U.S. Treasury believed that the British wanted $3 billion in gold at $35 an ounce. At that price American gold reserves were only $11 billion, and no one doubted that the British demand would initiate a scramble by other countries to convert dollars into gold as soon as possible before U.S. reserves ran out.

To deal with the crisis, and in general to seize control of the economic situation, Nixon outlined a "New Economic Policy." In a dramatic televised speech he announced that the United States would sever the link between the dollar and gold, allowing the greenback to "float," or find its own value in financial markets. The president also imposed a three-month freeze on wages and prices, to be followed by a system of controls that was supposed to break the spiral of rising wages and prices that had kept inflation high even as demand stagnated. Finally, Nixon announced that the government would stimulate the economy more aggressively, expanding outlays and cutting interest rates further.

Implementing these measures took time. In December 1971, after long talks with the other industrial democracies, the United States raised the official price of gold to $38, effectively devaluing the dollar by 8.6 percent. This, officials hoped, would make exports cheaper and imports more expensive, allowing the United States to rebuild its trade surplus. Washington did not, however, resume converting dollars held by other governments into gold, even at the higher price. In the spring of 1972 the administration finally forced reluctant labor unions to limit raises to 5.5 percent a year, a level consistent with lower inflation. Meanwhile interest rates fell and the money supply expanded substantially, even as Washington ran a hefty $23.4 billion deficit, slightly larger than the previous year despite stronger economic growth.

In the short run Nixon got exactly what he wanted. The economy grew at a strong 5.5 percent in 1972 while consumer prices rose only 3.2 percent, the lowest increase since 1967. By the end of the year, unemployment had fallen to 5 percent. Surging demand permitted companies to operate their facilities at fuller capacity, securing sharp improvements in productivity that allowed them to pay higher wages, limit price hikes, and still boost profits an average of 15 percent. Prosperity was one of several factors that contributed to President Nixon's landslide reelection in 1972.

Despite these successes, the president's economic advisers looked forward to 1973 with concern. On the international level, the balance of trade had actually deteriorated over 1972—imports exceeding exports by $5 billion. In part this was because a devaluation affects trade only gradually—exporters must develop new markets, and those competing against imports must expand capacity. In the meantime, higher prices for imports and lower ones for exports may actually expand a deficit. Nevertheless some government officials and economists began to fear that the devaluation had not been large enough to restore the balance of payments to equilibrium. At home, concern centered on inflation. As the economy grew, production in many industries was approaching capacity. If demand continued to expand, shortages would develop—indeed, that was already the case in agriculture.

Controls might be able to force companies and unions to keep prices and wages stable if demand was weak, but experience suggested that they could not contain inflation created by shortages. To meet this challenge the government would have to use monetary and fiscal policy to limit demand. All in all, repeating the relatively good performance of 1972 would be difficult.

3

The Great Stagflation

IN 1973 the long postwar boom ended. A generation of prosperity gave way to a decade of stagnation characterized by sluggish growth and steadily rising prices. At first most Americans considered the crisis a passing phenomenon that required, at most, a few minor adjustments. Gradually, however, they realized that improvement would require significant changes in economic life, and they inaugurated major reforms.

A GREAT CRASH

Between 1973 and 1975 the United States lurched from one disaster to another. The Watergate scandal forced Richard Nixon from office and seriously weakened the institution of the presidency. The Vietnam War ended in defeat. For many Americans, however, economic problems were paramount.

The period started with another devaluation of the dollar. The large U.S. payments deficit in 1972 had damaged confidence in the greenback, and in January 1973 currency traders sold hundreds of millions of dollars. The industrial democracies, unable or unwilling to buy all these greenbacks, quickly agreed to devalue the dollar by 10 percent against the currencies of Western Europe and Japan. This failed to halt the crisis, and heavy sales of greenbacks resumed in March. Mystified and frustrated, the industrial democracies did the only thing they could—withdrawing from financial markets and allowing their currencies to "float."

Although no one had planned this outcome, it represented the logical culmination of recent financial history. Years of devaluation and revaluation involving not only the dollar but the currencies of all the industrial democracies had demolished confidence in the very idea of currency pegs—and in financial markets, confidence is vital. Billions of dollars change hands every day in currency markets. If all currency traders sell simultaneously, no central bank or group of central banks can absorb the flood of money. By 1973 most traders had concluded that governments considered devaluation the best—or at least the easiest—way to resolve a large payment deficit. Knowing this, they sold the currency of any country facing a substantial deficit, effectively forcing the devaluation they anticipated. This atmosphere left governments with three alternatives: floating, living with regular financial crises, or adopting drastic measures such as higher interest rates, sharp cuts in government spending, and strict controls on foreign exchange to defend pegs and reassure financial markets. Not surprisingly in light of the alternatives, they chose the first option.

From Washington's perspective, floating worked fairly well. The dollar stabilized about 10 percent below its 1972 peg—that is, where it had stood after the January devaluation. The March crisis was largely one of the system of fixed pegs, not of the dollar per se. The cheaper dollar, coupled with strong demand abroad, encouraged a boom in exports that left the United States with a solid current account surplus for 1973. But other problems soon eclipsed this success.

In early 1973 prices surged forward in the United States. The Nixon administration relaxed wage-price controls in January, ending enforcement in all but a few crucial sectors. The president and most of his advisers had never liked controls, considering them a political expedient at odds with the American tradition of free enterprise. Now with Nixon safely reelected, the administration could dispose of them. Controls had accomplished their chief objective, slowing wage increases to a level consistent with relatively low inflation. Unfortunately, relaxation came at a bad time. Rapid economic growth throughout the world in 1972 had created strong demand for every sort of commodity and put upward pressure on prices. The devaluation of the dollar made a difficult situation worse by effectively reducing the price of American goods 10 percent for foreigners, who rushed in to buy. In the first half of 1973, strong demand pushed wholesale prices up at a whopping 20 percent annual rate while consumer prices increased at more than an 8 percent rate.

Political factors complicated the situation. Inevitably in light of the chronology of events, many Americans blamed the relaxation of controls for rising prices and called for their reimposition. The developing Watergate scandal was sapping the president's support, making him eager for a political coup that would repair his standing. In the spring of 1973 Nixon capped the prices of meat and domestically produced oil, which had advanced particularly fast, but this had little impact on overall conditions. In June he tried again, imposing a sixty-day freeze on all prices. The president's economic advisers generally opposed the move, warning that it would do more harm than good. They conceded that in 1971, when rising wages were pushing prices higher, controls had represented an effective response to inflation. But 1973 was different. The country simply did not have enough goods to go around at current prices, and controls would merely translate inflation into shortage. The analysis was unimpeachable, but as was often the case with Nixon, political rather than economic considerations guided his policy.

As Nixon's advisers had predicted, the freeze worked badly.

Some producers refused to sell at prices set by the government, holding goods back from the market. In other cases the freeze forced businesses to operate at a loss. Although the prices of raw materials had increased, some firms had yet to raise their own charges, either because they were waiting to see if higher costs persisted or because they simply had not yet gotten around to it. Nixon had to abandon the freeze well before sixty days had elapsed, putting in its stead a new regime designed to gradually phase out all controls. With the important exception of petroleum, regulation of wages and prices finally ended by the spring of 1974.

These events not only further eroded Nixon's popularity but turned public opinion decisively against wage-price controls. Despite controls, inflation had intensified between 1971 and 1973. The public would remember this episode and refuse to support another such experiment, even when inflation rose to even higher levels later in the decade.

After the summer of 1973 the Nixon administration fought inflation with what Treasury Secretary George Shultz called "that old-time religion": fiscal and monetary restraint. Heavy demand was driving prices higher, and the only solution was to reduce demand. Unfortunately, because of the developing Watergate scandal, the administration lacked the political strength to secure large cuts in federal spending from Congress. It did manage to limit new outlays for fiscal 1974, holding the deficit to $6.1 billion. But in an economy already operating near its capacity, this had little impact. The Federal Reserve took strong measures, however, raising interest rates to record levels. By August 1973 the prime rate stood at 10 percent, and in the summer of 1974 it hit 12 percent. Eventually this had an effect. Home construction fell from more than 2 million units in 1972 and 1973 to 1.3 million units in 1974 and 1.2 million in 1975. Overall investment declined 8 percent in 1974 and 18 percent in 1975.

The jump in prices during the first half of 1973 reflected errors made in 1972. Then, the Nixon administration and the Federal Reserve had stimulated the economy even though it was already operating close to full capacity. The government ran a large deficit and the Fed kept interest rates stable even as the demand for loans grew, permitting rapid expansion of the money supply. In an economy with little spare capacity, such measures inevitably stoked inflation. In part this policy reflected political factors—Nixon was determined to have prosperity while he ran for reelection. More important, controls concealed developing shortages. Usually economists pay close attention to prices in critical sectors for signs that the economy is approaching its physical capacity, but controls prevented vendors from raising prices in response to shortage, effectively muting such warnings. Changes in the labor market exacerbated the risk of miscalculation. Most economists still assumed that 4 or 4.5 percent unemployment represented full employment. So they concluded that, with unemployment above 5 percent in 1972, the economy still had substantial idle resources. In fact, however, the growing willingness of American workers to change jobs—in part a reflection of the number of young people ("baby boomers") entering the workplace for the first time—meant that 5.5 percent unemployment probably represented full employment. There was no economic "slack." Finally, the logic of controls made it difficult for the Fed to raise interest rates. With other prices fixed, it was hard to justify increasing the cost of money.

In the fall of 1973 the Arab oil embargo added a new dimension to the country's economic woes. In October, Israel and its Arab neighbors went to war for the fourth time in twenty-five years. Unlike the previous three conflicts, in which Israel triumphed easily, the Arabs won some important victories at the outset of the 1973 war. The Israelis desperately requested military aid from the United States, which Washington granted, and with this help repulsed their opponents. But U.S. intervention infuriated the Arab world, which included several leading oil exporters: Saudi Arabia, Iraq, Kuwait, and Libya. These countries terminated all oil shipments to the United States and cut their total output by 5 percent a month. Before the embargo the world's oil fields were already operating at capacity to supply consumers, so these cutbacks created a severe, across-the-board shortage.

Worldwide panic ensued. Almost everyone felt the embargo—motorists could not find gasoline, homeowners paid more to heat their homes, and companies that used oil scrambled for supplies. Responses to the crisis were not always rational. Some American motorists became obsessed with keeping their gas tanks full, forming long lines at service stations to "top off" whenever their gas gauge registered less than full. In Japan, attention for some reason focused on toilet paper, which became the object of widespread hoarding. Deft negotiations by the Nixon administration restored the flow of oil in the spring of 1974, but previous conditions did not return. In 1974 the Organization of Petroleum Exporting Countries (OPEC), which consisted of the governments of most of the oil-exporting countries, set the official price of oil at $11.65 a barrel. As recently as 1970 it had been $1.80.

The energy crisis reflected political and economic trends in the oil industry. After 1945 the leading international oil companies had developed huge new oil fields in the Middle East, and for two decades their chief problem had been selling the resulting flood of petroleum. They had offered oil at low, stable prices to encourage consumption, which had boomed. By 1970, however, consumption had finally caught up with and surpassed output. This alone would have forced prices higher, but political factors reinforced the trend. Producer countries increasingly took control of the oil fields from foreign companies. At first the

companies had split the earnings from production with governments, but in the late 1960s attitudes changed. Authorities
wanted more of the profits from the oil fields, and nationaliza-
tion offered political dividends by demonstrating producer
countries' power and pride. By 1975 all the major oil exporters—
Venezuela, Saudi Arabia, Kuwait, Iraq, Iran, Libya, Indonesia,
Nigeria, and others—had nationalized their oil fields. National-
ization greatly increased the power of OPEC, allowing it to set
the price of oil, at least as long as the market remained tight. Decisions about oil prices now became as much a political as an economic matter. OPEC increased charges not simply to balance
supply and demand but also to demonstrate its power and to impose a vague and not disinterested concept of economic justice.

The oil shortage intensified inflation and tipped the American
economy into recession. Oil prices are a key component of the
cost of energy, which is basic to the price of almost everything.
Petroleum is also the raw material for plastics, which go into a
vast array of other products. The impact did not always appear
immediately—it often took a year or more for higher oil prices
to filter through the economy. But in 1974 consumer prices increased 12 percent. Higher oil prices also slowed growth. The
shortage of energy and raw materials (petroleum, plastics) forced
many companies to reduce output. More broadly, higher oil
prices operated like a huge tax on the economy, reducing the
purchasing power of consumers and business.

Although the economy began to shrink in late 1973, speculative investment delayed the full impact. Throughout 1973 individuals and firms spent heavily on commercial real estate and
commodities, whose value usually kept up with the general price
level. Companies also purchased raw materials and expanded
inventories well beyond their immediate needs on the assumption that prices would continue rising. Credit financed much of
this activity. Although interest rates were extremely high, the

prospect of large gains made borrowers willing to pay. With inflation at 8 to 10 percent, interest rates of 8 to 10 percent did not seem exorbitant.

Throughout the 1970s this divergence between "nominal" and "real" interest rates distorted monetary policy. Whereas politicians and the public at large generally focused on the cost of money (nominal rates), short-term borrowers focused on the difference between interest rates and inflation (real rates). Retailers, for example, were happy to borrow at 10 percent to finance inventory appreciating at 12 percent. Real interest rates were not an infallible guide to policy, because in evaluating rates long-term borrowers used different criteria than short-term borrowers. Nevertheless a monetary policy that at first glance appeared restrictive often proved in an atmosphere of inflation to be expansionary.

Over the course of 1974 the speculative boom collapsed. Higher oil prices choked off consumer spending even as the Federal Reserve raised interest rates to unprecedented levels, with the prime rate at 12 percent. This was finally high enough to discourage borrowing, particularly for home mortgages. A homeowner will find the appreciation of his or her property at 10 to 12 percent a year gratifying but must still come up with money to pay the mortgage every month—not an easy feat at interest rates of 12 percent. Over 1974 most companies recognized that inventories and stocks of raw materials were grossly out of proportion to sales and reduced their own purchases to restore balance. In the fall, companies began to cut back steeply on investment; electric utilities alone reduced construction schedules by $22 billion.

By late 1974 the gradual economic retreat of late 1973 had become a rout. The sharp decline of commodity, real estate, and stock prices saddled businesses and financial institutions with heavy losses. In the summer of 1974 the Franklin National Bank of New York, an institution with more than $4 billion in assets, declared bankruptcy—by far the largest bank failure to that time in U.S. history. Although still solvent, leading institutions like Chase Manhattan and Citibank incurred substantial losses from loan defaults. But American workers bore the brunt of the downturn. Sharp reductions in investment led to massive layoffs in construction and manufacturing that quickly spread to consumer industries. In December 1974 alone, one million lost their jobs. By May 1975 the unemployment rate was 9 percent, by far the highest level since the Great Depression.

Political crisis made a coordinated government response to the collapse impossible. The Watergate scandal forced President Nixon to concentrate all his energies on political survival, and the president's fate obsessed Congress no less than Nixon himself. His resignation in August 1974 improved the atmosphere somewhat. But the new president, Republican Gerald Ford, had to assemble a new administration, and the Congress, dominated by Democrats who had just forced one president from office, was reluctant to cooperate with him.

The Federal Reserve did act, however. During the fall of 1974, as financial problems and declining investment made it clear that the economy was in severe recession, it cut interest rates sharply. By the spring of 1975 the prime rate was down to 7 percent. Pointing to anemic growth in the money supply over the winter of 1974–1975, economists from Paul Samuelson to Milton Friedman argued that the central bank had reacted too slowly. This charge has truth—more aggressive easing, initiated earlier, might have mitigated the downturn. The collapse, however, had its basis in real factors, not in a shortage of money. Speculative investment had left companies with far more inventory and capacity than they needed, and monetary policy could not alter these unpleasant facts.

Despite talk of a second Great Depression, the economy recovered over the summer of 1975. The Federal Reserve made sure that troubled but basically sound companies had access to credit, and once companies had sold off the stocks of raw materials and inventories accumulated in 1973 and 1974 as a hedge against inflation, they resumed buying. Lower interest rates encouraged a resurgence of investment, which increased by 20 percent in 1976. The federal government assisted recovery by cutting taxes $20 billion, most of which went to individuals in the form of tax rebates. Overall Washington ran a deficit of $53 billion in fiscal 1975 and $73 billion in 1976, a total of 3.3 and 4.1 percent of GDP, respectively—the highest since World War II. All of this combined to drive a healthy if unspectacular recovery that by the end of 1975 had reduced unemployment to 7.5 percent.

Yet inflation remained high. Consumer prices rose 9 percent in 1975 despite the downturn. In part this reflected the delayed effect of higher oil prices, but the problem went deeper. Years of rising prices had institutionalized inflation. Union contracts, which usually extended three years, contained increases designed to compensate for anticipated inflation. In some instances agreements included cost-of-living adjustments that automatically raised wages in line with consumer prices. Although union contracts covered less than a third of the workforce, they set pay scales in many sectors. Employers granted large raises on the assumption that they could pass increases on to consumers in the form of higher prices, and consumers paid higher prices on the assumption that rising wages would cover the expense. Even in the absence of any shortages, expectations of inflation drove prices and wages higher. Improvement in this pattern would require considerable changes in attitudes as well as in economic conditions.

Rising prices created a variety of problems. Those who lived on fixed incomes—pensions, annuities—suffered greatly as the purchasing power of their money declined. Long-term interest rates rose to compensate for rising prices—no one would lend at 8 percent if they expected prices to rise at a 10 percent rate—increasing the immediate cost of housing and investment in new plants. Inflation also distorted corporate decision-making, largely by understating the cost of depreciation—the regular wear and tear on equipment. (Companies each year set aside a portion of the value of their buildings and equipment to compensate for depreciation, an expense that is deducted from earnings.) Tax law required that firms calculate this in terms of the original cost of equipment, not the inflated cost of replacing it. As a result, companies often failed to make adequate provision for this important expense, an omission with dangerous long-term implications because depreciation was an important source of money for capital spending.

In theory the Federal Reserve could halt inflation simply by refusing to create money to finance rising prices, but in practice difficulties abounded. Such a policy would almost certainly create a deep recession. Inflation had considerable momentum, as expectations of rising prices led companies to raise prices and wages regularly. If the money supply did not expand in line with such expectations, first sales and then employment would fall because people would lack the cash with which to buy. This would generate strong political resistance. Although everyone professed to abhor inflation, every increase in interest rates during the 1970s, no matter how limited, evoked denunciations from many quarters, most notably Congress.

Despite a slow start, the Ford administration did develop a coherent economic program that emphasized reducing inflation. It sought to ease inflationary pressures and expectations with monetary and fiscal restraint. During the last eighteen months of the Ford administration, the Federal Reserve, which worked closely with the president and his advisers, held the growth of the most basic measure of the money supply to an annual rate of 4 to 6 percent, raising rates if necessary to hit this target. Meanwhile the president fought with Congress to contain spending. Democrats, who had large majorities in both houses of the legislature, argued for more public spending to reduce the high level of unemployment, but Ford and his supporters contended that inflation was the more immediate problem and the real cause of the recession. Lasting prosperity, they claimed, required stable prices. Besides, Washington was already running huge deficits because of the decline in revenues caused by the recession. Although the administration failed to substantially reduce spending, it did manage to avoid large new commitments.

Ford's policies yielded modest gains. Prices rose a little less than 6 percent in 1976, though unemployment remained stubbornly high at more than 7 percent. But the prosperity of the 1950s and 1960s still conditioned public expectations, and by this standard the Ford administration fell short. In 1976 Democrat Jimmy Carter won the presidency—and responsibility for righting the American economy.

A New International Regime?

Although the world had abandoned fixed exchange rates in 1973, most of the structures and procedures associated with Bretton Woods endured. The IMF and the World Bank continued to operate. Individuals and companies could still easily convert the money of one country into that of another, though now the price fluctuated. Most important, cooperation among the industrial democracies persisted and even intensified. Despite frictions, they still operated on the assumption that their economies would prosper or languish together.

Nevertheless the shift to floating exchange rates did entail major changes. In many ways floating made the management of economic policy much easier. Provided that a country was willing to tolerate some movement in the value of its currency, it could set fiscal and monetary policy solely with reference to domestic conditions. The situation of the late 1950s, when the United States kept interest rates high and spending down, in part to protect the dollar's value in international markets even though the domestic economy was sluggish, need not repeat itself. Governments could also safely abandon controls on the movement of capital over borders—regulations both vexing and hard to enforce. After 1973 Washington scrapped the interest equalization tax as well as its ban on the private ownership of gold.

Still, floating imposed burdens. Some economists, such as Milton Friedman, had argued that floating rates would automatically resolve payments imbalances. A country with a deficit would find its money depreciating, which would encourage exports and discourage imports; a nation with a surplus would experience the reverse. In fact, though, there was no guarantee that currency values would gravitate toward levels that would provide a balance on the current account. Currency trading was large and growing fast—by the early 1990s transactions in currency markets averaged a staggering $1 trillion a day, many times greater than the actual exchange of goods and services. Currency traders sought short-term gains, taking advantage of shifts in currency values and differences in interest rates between countries. For example, if interest rates in Germany were higher than in the United States, traders would borrow dollars, buy deutschemarks, and invest the money in Germany. Their profit would be the difference in interest rates. The "correct" value of a currency over the long run—the level that would yield a balance on the current account—was of little interest to them. Government actions might produce perverse results. A country that raised interest rates to combat inflation might find its currency appreciating despite a large current account deficit created in part by rising domestic prices. Floating could also create problems for firms operating across international borders. Currency values have a huge impact on the cost of imports, the revenue from exports, and the profits of foreign subsidiaries, and floating made it that much more difficult for companies to plan for the future.

Governments and companies devised various measures to manage these problems. Political authorities expanded international consultation, most notably inaugurating in 1976 the annual Group of Seven summits (among Britain, Canada, France, West Germany, Italy, Japan, and the United States). Governments would intervene jointly in currency markets to support or force down a currency whose value seemed grossly out of line with economic realities. The industrial democracies and the IMF also assisted countries facing declines in the value of their currencies so large as to threaten their external trade and financial solvency.

The energy crisis provided the occasion for the first rescue operations under the new order. By sharply raising the price of crude oil, OPEC threw the rest of the world into deficit. The United States, which still supplied half its own oil, and Germany and Japan, which both had large trade surpluses, managed the problem on their own, but others were not so fortunate. In 1974 the other industrial democracies loaned money to Italy to finance its oil imports, and in 1976 they did the same for Britain. In the latter case they advanced the money through the IMF, which extracted promises that London would reduce its government deficit and restrain the growth of the money supply, with the idea of cutting inflation as well as the British payments deficit. This operation became the model for later rescues, which generally involved less-developed countries rather than the industrial democracies.

Under the new regime, private interests played a greater role in international finance than under Bretton Woods. This devel-

opment reflected a trend under way long before 1973. The Great
Depression and World War II had largely ended private investment across borders, and the architects of Bretton Woods had assumed that in the future most international investment would
come from government institutions like the World Bank. But
after 1945 private investment across borders, in the form of both
direct investment by companies and investors' purchase of securities, had gradually expanded. By the 1970s private investors
were ready to take a role in managing the system. Most notably,
banks financed the deficits of third world countries without oil
reserves. These countries required far less money than the industrial countries, but considering the smaller size of their economies and their less-developed financial markets, they faced
perhaps greater difficulties in adjusting to higher oil prices. Oil-
producing countries, however, found that higher prices left them
with far more cash then they could readily spend. For the moment they left the money on deposit with Western banks, chiefly
those in the United States. Because the recession had cut the demand for loans at home, U.S. institutions had trouble finding
borrowers for the money, and they happily granted developing
countries credits to finance oil imports.

The process, known as "recycling," raised many concerns.
How would borrowers, often very poor countries, pay the interest on these loans, much less the principal? Would the money go
to finance development, or would it wind up in the secret bank
accounts of corrupt officials? Nevertheless those involved had
reason to prefer such credits to loans from, say, the IMF. The
banks earned substantial profits—at least for the moment—and
borrowers avoided the conditions that an institution like the
IMF might impose.

Private firms also developed an array of financial devices to
manage the uncertainty created by floating exchange rates. They
bought and sold currency through forward contracts or pur-

chased options, tactics that allowed them to hedge against fluctuations in currency rates. But such devices have limits. They are
not free; forward markets extend no more than a year into the
future; and they provide no help at all if exchange rates are already at an inappropriate level.

The New Regulation

In the late 1960s and early 1970s the American government imposed a new class of regulation on business. Most federal
regulations had sought to control "natural" monopolies, prevent
underhanded competition, and ban destructive competition.
Such measures assumed that structural factors distorted the
workings of markets, making direct government intervention
necessary. New measures sought to remedy "externalities," the
noneconomic results of business activity. Most firms, for instance,
had no economic interest one way or another in the amount of
smoke their factories emitted into the atmosphere—it was external to their business calculations. Such pollution, however, could
have grave social consequences. Smog blanketed many American cities, threatening the health of residents. Unrestricted
dumping of sewage and industrial waste had made bodies
of water like the Chicago River and Lake Erie toxic. The pesti-
cide DDT threatened birds of prey like hawks and eagles with
extinction. Thousands of Americans died every year of work-
related injuries or ailments.

Recognition of these problems during the 1960s created pressure for action that culminated in extensive legislation in the
early 1970s. During the Nixon administration, Congress created
the Environmental Protection Agency (EPA) to regulate air and
water quality as well as the safety of various chemicals; the Occu-
pational Health and Safety Administration (OSHA) to improve
safety in the workplace; and the Consumer Product Safety Com-

mission (CPSC) to protect buyers of goods and services. The Food and Drug Administration (FDA), which had existed since the 1900s, also substantially tightened its regulations, requiring drug makers to demonstrate not only the safety of their products but also their effectiveness.

In many cases regulation led to substantial improvements. Restrictions on air pollution—particularly the installation of catalytic converters in automobiles—led to sharp declines in smog in many cities, and limits on dumping allowed marine life to return to Lake Erie. A ban on DDT permitted the population of hawks and eagles to recover. OSHA requirements eliminated cotton dust from textile mills, freeing workers from the crippling ailment known as brown lung.

Progress carried a price, however. "Scrubbers" that removed sulfur, a major pollutant, from the smoke of power plants were extremely expensive, consuming 2 to 5 percent of a plant's output of electricity. Facilities to treat sewage were even costlier. Farmers had to switch to pesticides that were less potent and more expensive than DDT. Legislators made little attempt to make sure that the benefits of regulation justified the costs. Herbert Stein, the head of Nixon's CEA, wrote that attempts to balance costs and benefits "foundered on a tide of congressional demagoguery and sentimentality plus bureaucratic zeal." To many environmentalists, the advantages of safety and a clean environment were beyond price. Rules sought to prescribe what companies ought to do in almost every possible circumstance, creating an incredibly complex and rigid system. For example, by 1976 the EPA had devised a total of 492 different guidelines governing water pollution and had issued 45,000 permits regulating plants that emitted such pollutants. OSHA regulations occasionally shaded into the ridiculous, setting rules for how employees should climb ladders and for the shape of toilet seats.

By the late 1970s such regulation constituted a major griev-

ance by businesses large and small against the federal government. Their resentment was not disinterested—they objected to
the expense of such regulation and took little notice of the benefits it yielded society. But it was true that in some cases the benefits of regulations had not justified the expense, and that in other
instances the country could have achieved the same ends at lower
cost.

THE CARTER ADMINISTRATION

The experience of Jimmy Carter, who became president
in January 1977, demonstrates the limits of good intentions and
hard work. A former governor of Georgia, Carter won first the
Democratic nomination and then the presidency in 1976 by pos-
ing as someone who, by virtue of his position outside Washington's power structure, could restore integrity to a federal
government discredited by the Vietnam War and the Watergate
scandal. But he had only a vague program of reform beyond a
yearning for "good government," and no large group of supporters from whom to draw staff and ideas. For both he relied on a
small cadre of advisers from Georgia and Democrats long en-
trenched in Washington.

They had little new to offer in the way of economic policy.
Carter's chief economic advisers had served in the Kennedy and
Johnson administrations and still thought in terms of "fine tuning." They remained wedded to the Phillips Curve, which postu-
lated a trade-off between inflation and unemployment, and some
were willing to tolerate higher inflation if they could push unemployment down. Congressional Democrats, who enjoyed solid
majorities in both chambers, were even less flexible. As Carter
himself said of them, "All they knew about it [economics] was
stimulus and Great Society programs."

Carter's advisers believed that they confronted a situation similar to that faced by the Kennedy administration in 1961. Like Kennedy, they inherited an economy that still had not fully recovered from recession, and they thought that because the country had idle resources, fiscal and monetary stimulus could increase output without intensifying inflation. But the situation differed from 1961 in crucial respects. Then, prices had been stable, forced into line by four years of fiscal and monetary restraint. In 1977 prices were increasing at more than 6 percent annually, and years of inflation had led Americans to assume that prices would continue to rise. Stimulus might well translate into inflation rather than higher production. Moreover the Kennedy administration had been able to use wage-price guidelines to contain inflation, whereas the disappointing experience with controls in the early 1970s had rendered such measures politically impossible for Carter.

The Carter administration found that its desire to stimulate the economy without fueling inflation pulled it in two directions, making a consistent policy impossible. Every winter, in response to statistics that suggested growth was slowing, the president announced a package of spending increases and tax cuts. Every summer, in response to more rapid price increases, he announced a plan to balance the federal budget.

Nevertheless, on balance policy remained stimulative. Although the economy expanded briskly in 1977 and 1978 and unemployment declined toward 6 percent, the federal deficit shrank only slowly because the president's sporadic interest in balancing the budget rarely had as strong an impact as did his intermittent calls for new spending and tax cuts. Perhaps more important, the money supply grew rapidly, reflecting strong demand for loans. Not only was the economy recovering, but because inflation was high and rising, people were willing to pay steep interest rates. To contain monetary growth and inflation, the Fed would have to increase substantially "real" interest rates, the gap between the price of money and the pace of inflation. As a practical matter, this would mean raising interest rates very aggressively, which the Fed failed to do. The money supply grew substantially between 1977 and 1980, and the rate of inflation rose in every year of Carter's administration.

Among economic issues, President Carter devoted his greatest attention to energy policy. Rising oil prices contributed mightily to inflation and slowed economic growth, and the president and many other Americans feared that dependence on imported petroleum threatened national security. Carter himself declared the matter "the moral equivalent of war." In 1973, in response to public pressure, President Nixon had imposed controls on the price of domestically produced crude, preventing it from increasing in line with the price of oil abroad. These regulations continued despite the demise of general wage-price controls, and by 1977 oil from established wells in Texas or Oklahoma sold for less than half the world price. This policy had numerous drawbacks. By keeping oil prices low, it discouraged conservation. By way of compensation, Congress tried to impose conservation by law, most notably requiring automakers to raise the average mileage of their cars to twenty miles per gallon by 1980. Such measures had an impact, but they lacked the pervasive effect of higher prices. Controls also discouraged new drilling. Oil from new wells was allowed to fetch a higher price than that from established wells, but this was still short of the world price. Expensive or risky drilling, which might have made economic sense at the world price, was not always appealing at the lower domestic one. And the distinction between old and new oil was, in practice, confusing, inviting misunderstanding and even fraud.

By 1977 almost everyone who had seriously studied the matter agreed that controls on domestic oil did more harm than good. But officials feared the inflationary impact of allowing domestic oil to rise to the world price. Political factors were also an obstacle. Decontrol would lead to higher prices, at least in the short run, and no one wanted to pay more for gasoline and heating oil. And deregulation would further fatten the earnings of the unpopular oil companies, whose profits had ballooned with the price of oil. The Carter administration sought to finesse the matter. It devised a program that combined gradual deregulation with subsidies to encourage both conservation and the development of alternative sources of energy—measures that would soften the shock of rising prices. But Congress acted slowly, taking a year to pass Carter's energy program and amending it substantially in the process.

The new legislation was barely in place when disaster struck. The Iranian revolution of 1978–1979 temporarily halted production in that country's vast oil fields. Remembering the Arab oil embargo, buyers panicked and began purchasing all the gasoline and oil they could find, thereby creating the shortage they feared. OPEC took advantage of the situation, doubling its posted price for oil, and by 1980 a barrel of crude cost close to $40. Ironically, oil production actually outpaced consumption during this time—higher prices and shortages reflected panic and hoarding, not an imbalance of supply and demand. Nevertheless the higher cost of oil worsened inflation. Consumer prices rose more than 10 percent in 1979 and almost 14 percent in 1980. Rising prices created panic. Emblematically, the price of gold approached $1,000 an ounce, nearly thirty times its 1968 level. People wanted an asset that would hold its value, and gold had traditionally offered that. Meanwhile oil shortages slowed economic growth. The most famous casualty was the automaker Chrysler, which in 1980 required loan guarantees from the federal government to avoid bankruptcy.

Meanwhile the dollar fell alarmingly. After holding fairly steady since 1973, the dollar began to fall against the currencies of the other industrial democracies in 1977. This reflected the large U.S. deficit on the current account—over $10 billion—as well as the perception that inflation was increasing in the United States, both of which pointed toward a cheaper dollar. Initially the Carter administration ignored the problem, judging the decline a stimulus to exports and, as such, a solution to the trade deficit. But in the second half of 1978 the administration realized that the situation might spin out of control. In particular it was concerned that the falling dollar would make domestic inflation worse by raising both the cost of imports and the demand for exportable goods. In 1979 Washington persuaded the industrial democracies to launch a huge operation to prop up the dollar, buying $30 billion on the open market. The federal government also issued bonds denominated in foreign currencies, Japanese yen and German deutschemarks—the only such obligations ever issued by the U.S. government. These bond issues raised money with which Washington bought dollars and, more important, reassured traders that the U.S. government was serious about defending the greenback because a further fall in the dollar's value would substantially increase the cost of purchasing yen and deutschemarks to pay interest on these bonds.

Policy shifted decisively in 1979 when President Carter installed Paul Volcker as chairman of the Federal Reserve Board. He had vast experience as a government official and banker, and Carter appointed him in part to reassure financial markets. Volcker was determined to break inflation. He realized, however, that the matter involved not only economic but political and psychological factors. Expectations of inflation had played an important role in driving prices up, with unions, consumers, and companies all basing decisions on the assumption that prices would continue to increase. Because everyone raised wages and prices in anticipation of inflation, they created the thing they expected. Somehow Volcker had to convince people that inflation would not continue.

Monetarism offered him the device he needed. Since 1970, when Arthur Burns had become chairman, the Fed had paid close attention to the money supply in setting policy. But it had taken interest rates into account too. In October 1979 Volcker announced that henceforth the Fed would ignore interest rates entirely and instead target only monetary growth. The advantages were chiefly political. On one hand, by adhering to a target the Fed lent credibility to its drive to limit inflation. On the other hand, Volcker believed that any effective anti-inflation policy would require very high interest rates, which would be unpopular. The Fed's new approach would allow the central bank to raise the cost of credit to much higher levels without explicitly adopting a policy of high interest rates. The Fed simply limited the supply of money and let interest rates go where they would—which in this case was up. Throughout 1980 the prime rate averaged a staggering 15 percent—high even after taking inflation into account. Early in the year the economy fell into recession.

DEREGULATION

The Carter administration did make a lasting contribution to economic policy by initiating deregulation. Since the 1930s—earlier in some cases—the federal government had regulated transportation, utilities, and finance, setting prices and terms of service. Together, regulated sectors accounted for as much as a quarter of the GDP. Pressure for reform came from several quarters. By the 1970s most economists had concluded that regulation too often failed to serve the public. In transportation, government control over pricing and service kept prices and costs high. Critics described the system as a government-sponsored cartel that exploited consumers, discouraged competition, and allowed inefficient firms to survive. Utility regulation, which rested on rate-of-return calculations, had similar results.

Because total investment was the base from which regulators set rates, firms had incentives for unnecessary capital spending. In other cases, regulations imposed crippling inefficiencies on business. The price that companies could charge for natural gas was not high enough to justify exploration for new reserves, and during the severe winters of 1976–1977 and 1977–1978, shortages appeared. At government insistence, AT&T (the Bell System) charged high long-distance rates to subsidize cheap local tariffs. By the 1970s this policy had attracted challengers—most notably Microwave Communications Inc. (MCI)—who eroded AT&T's long-distance business, which financed all its other services. To attract money as interest rates rose, Savings & Loans had to offer depositors higher returns, but most of their assets remained in fixed-rate mortgages made years earlier at low rates. By 1980 their losses had reached disastrous levels. Compelling as these specific cases were, however, broader concerns made deregulation a priority. Inflation was the chief economic problem of the late 1970s, and politicians were receptive to anything that might slow its pace without increasing unemployment. Deregulation, by making the economy more efficient, promised to do this.

Deregulation proceeded piecemeal. The Securities and Exchange Commission ended minimum commissions on stock trades in the mid-1970s. Legislation allowed railroads, airlines, and truckers to make their own decisions on pricing and service starting in 1980. In 1982 AT&T settled a long-standing anti-trust suit with the federal government, agreeing to divest its local phone companies—the "baby bells"—and to concentrate solely on long distance. In the latter market AT&T would set its own prices in competition with firms like MCI and Sprint. In the late 1970s and early 1980s the government gradually ended price controls on natural gas and made pipelines common carriers that were required to offer all shippers the same price and service. Over the same period Washington permitted banks to offer cus-

tomers a broader variety of services, like interest-bearing check-
ing (NOW) accounts, and state legislatures gradually repealed
restrictions against out-of-state ownership of local banks, allowing institutions to operate across state boundaries.

Except in transportation, the term "deregulation" was a mis-
nomer. In most cases regulation did not vanish but rather took a
new form. Whereas before the 1970s regulation had replaced
markets with administrative dictation, deregulation usually involved a conscious effort to create and nurture markets—as the
historian Richard Vietor put it, deregulation represented "contrived competition." For instance, natural gas pipelines by law
had to carry the gas of all customers at the same price. A firm
that controlled both wells and pipelines could not offer consumers a reduction in transit fees in exchange for buying its
product. Similarly, local phone companies had to give consumers
equal access to all long-distance carriers.

In time, deregulation had a huge impact on the American
economy. Airline fares fell sharply, allowing the number of passengers flying to rise from 297 million in 1980 to 466 million in
1990—a 57 percent increase. Long-distance telephone rates declined from 25 to 30 cents a minute in the 1970s to 5 to 10 cents a
minute in the 1990s, despite a substantial rise in the general price
level. Railroads began to earn solid profits carrying freight, allowing Washington to sell off Conrail in a public stock offering.

As is usually the case with any really large change, unexpected
outcomes abounded. Airlines and railroads (though not trucking) saw consolidation; by the end of the century three airlines
controlled over half of plane traffic, and four railroads managed
almost all the country's rail mileage. Deregulation had permitted
aggressive firms to exploit the economies of scale inherent in the
airline and railroad businesses to eliminate or take over rivals.
Trucking had fewer such economies and so remained decentral-
ized. Consolidation occurred in finance as well, with institutions

like the Bank of America, Citicorp, Morgan Chase, and Bank One taking over other banks until, by the end of the century, they served millions of customers in dozens of states.

Not everyone profited from deregulation. Unions in newly competitive sectors found that, whereas regulation had often allowed firms to take a cavalier attitude toward labor expenses, competition gave employers a strong incentive to limit their expenses. In particular, airlines saw a series of dramatic strikes in the 1980s and early 1990s as companies cut wages and workforces. Savings & Loans, which in the early 1980s received the authority to buy bonds and lend on commercial real estate, generally made a mess of these operations, with which they had little experience. The industry, weak in 1980, was bankrupt by 1990. Consumers of natural gas discovered that, although they benefited when gas prices fell, they paid larger bills when it increased.

Nevertheless on balance deregulation benefited the United States. Lower prices and better service were more common than the opposite. More important, key industries were free to experiment and innovate. They often made mistakes, but errors are an inevitable part of innovation. Regulation had largely frozen into place the structure of critical parts of American industry, something a dynamic economy cannot tolerate indefinitely.

THE REAGAN REVOLUTION

Ronald Reagan's election as president in 1980 represented, among other things, the culmination of demands for economic reform. In 1976 voters had elected Jimmy Carter in the hope that the conscientious application of traditional policies could right the economy. But such measures proved inadequate. Carter had eventually recognized the need for thoroughgoing change, but he reached this conclusion reluctantly and never secured the solid support of congressional Democrats. In 1980 Carter gave way to the Republican Reagan, who was genuinely enthusiastic about sweeping reform.

By 1980 economists of all intellectual persuasions agreed that the American economy faced long-term problems that required a new approach to policy. Increasingly they focused on produc- tivity, seeing inflation as much a symptom as a cause of the coun- try's problems. Throughout most of the postwar era, output per worker had increased at about 3 percent a year, allowing steady advances in living standards, corporate profits, and government spending. Starting in 1973, however, the annual increase slowed to less than 1 percent. But expectations built over a generation do not change quickly. Workers continued to expect the kinds of raises they had received in the 1950s and 1960s, and employers too often assumed they could afford to pay such hikes. Govern- ment officials continued to launch new programs, assuming that growth would provide needed revenues. Put simply, demands on the economy grew as fast as ever, but its ability to produce did not.

This put the Federal Reserve in a difficult position. By raising interest rates and limiting monetary growth it could refuse to fi- nance expectations. This would keep prices stable by denying the money to pay higher wages and prices but would create unem- ployment and bankruptcies. Or it could supply money in line with expectations, which, given the failure of supply to grow as fast as demand, would cause inflation. The Fed generally chose the latter course. Initially its leaders expected productivity to grow 3 percent a year and set policy accordingly, only realizing in the mid-1970s that the economic context had changed. Just as important, however, the Fed feared the political consequences of containing monetary expansion. Even modest attempts to slow monetary growth in the mid-1970s had sparked strong public re- sistance; a really tough program could be a political disaster for the central bank. By 1980, however, opinion was beginning to shift. Paul Volcker's tough anti-inflation policy owed much to his own strong personality, but it also reflected new public attitudes. The economic pain caused by inflation had reached a point where most Americans were willing to tolerate drastic measures to reduce it.

Simply taming inflation would not solve the basic problem. Higher living standards required higher productivity. And if the country could substantially increase output per worker, the task of reducing inflation would become that much simpler because companies could pay higher wages without increasing prices as much. Accordingly, economists began to emphasize policies designed to improve productivity. This "supply side" approach took the discipline of economics in a new direction, or at least in a direction largely ignored for several decades. Keynesians and monetarists, each in their own way, had concentrated on keeping the demand for goods and services at the optimal level. Given stable demand, they had assumed that supply would take care of itself. From the perspective of the late 1970s, this attitude was no longer sufficient.

Liberal economic thinkers such as Lester Thurow and Robert Reich saw government investment as the solution. As Thurow put it in his widely read 1980 book *The Zero-Sum Society,* "Solving our energy and growth problems demands that government get more heavily involved in the economy's major investment decisions. . . . Investment funds need to be more rapidly channeled from our sunset [mature] to sunrise [growing] industries. To compete we need the national equivalent of a corporate investment committee. Major investment decisions have become too important to be left to the private market alone." Thurow, Reich, and their intellectual allies drew inspiration from Japan's Ministry of International Trade and Industry (MITI), which had supposedly fueled Japan's impressive postwar growth by directing resources toward the most promising sectors of the economy. American advocates of this approach referred to their program as "industrial policy."

Although appealing, industrial policy was politically unrealistic. By the late 1970s the Vietnam War and the Watergate scandal had badly shaken public confidence in government, and the electorate was unlikely to embrace the sort of huge expansion in Washington's responsibilities implied by industrial policy. Nor was Congress likely to permit officials to finance industry without specific legislative authorization. Lawmakers could probably be expected to channel as much money as possible to their constituents, regardless of whether they worked in "sunrise" or "sunset" industries—industrial policy might well finance steel rather than semiconductors.

The intellectual problems were at least as serious. Japan, France, and South Korea had all pursued fairly successful industrial policies in part because they were in many ways economically backward when they started. They could look at the wealthiest countries, see what they had done, and imitate. The United States had no such obvious guide. Despite its problems, the nation was clearly at the forefront of computers and most other "sunrise" industries. The way forward was not clear, and there was no reason to think that government officials could chart it better than private managers and entrepreneurs. More important, industrial policy had little to say about services, which by 1980 constituted roughly three-quarters of the American economy. It would be impossible to increase real income without improving productivity in this area. Indeed, advocates of industrial policy rarely had any specific plans for government investment, instead confining themselves to generalities about "sunrise" industries. They assumed that if the government set up something like Thurow's investment committee, the correct de-

cisions would follow. In a sense, then, planning became a substitute for a plan.

Conservatives wanted to take the country in the opposite direction. They argued that excessive government spending, taxes,
and regulation had crippled business, accounting for anemic productivity growth. As President Reagan said in his first inaugural
address in 1981, "In this present [economic] crisis, government is
not the solution to our problem. Government is the problem."
The conservative program embraced not only deregulation, an
initiative with support in both parties, but relaxation of environmental and safety standards to cut the cost of doing business. It
also sought to reduce spending on social programs, limiting the
federal government's demand on national resources.

Tax reduction, however, constituted the centerpiece of conservative reform. The top rate on income taxes was still 70 percent,
and because of wage inflation, high rates took effect at a much
lower level of real (inflation-adjusted) income. High taxes discouraged innovation—why work hard and take risks when the
government would appropriate most of the gains? Reagan himself, at the apex of his movie career in the 1940s, had realized that
high taxes made it unprofitable for him to appear in more than
four films a year and had reduced his work schedule to that pace.
The problem was particularly acute in a period of economic
change and uncertainty like the 1970s and 1980s. If the dangers
associated with entrepreneurship increase, then society must
allow greater returns to the successful—at least if it is to maintain the same level of growth. Of course, people could avoid taxes
by putting money into tax shelters, but these rarely represented
the most productive investments—otherwise they would not
need tax-exempt status to attract money. A substantial tax cut
might well encourage greater enterprise and make investment
more efficient.

But the question remained: how to pay for tax cuts? Conservatives wanted to balance the federal budget, both as a matter of principle and to free up capital for private investment. Tax cuts would reduce revenue, making this task more difficult. Here the calculations of economist Arthur Laffer provided the intellectual basis for policy. He argued that by reducing income taxes 30 percent, the government would not only reduce the burden on citizens and business but would actually encourage an expansion of income large enough to pay for the cut. Laffer operated from an economic truism. Taxation inevitably discourages consumption of the article taxed. Levies on gasoline, for instance, reduce fuel consumption because they raise its price. Therefore any tax reduction that stops short of abolition will pay for itself, in part, by increasing consumption of the goods taxed. Laffer argued that the same was true of income. Income taxes deter some from working and lead others to employ tax shelters to evade levies. Tax cuts would reduce these incentives, and higher incomes would yield more revenue even if rates were lower. Laffer, however, never explained adequately why a 30 percent reduction in income taxes would necessarily increase gross income by 30 percent.

Conservative Republicans seized upon Laffer's idea, not because it was good economics but because it was good politics. During the 1970s the taxes paid by the average American had increased substantially. Between 1971 and 1981 Social Security taxes increased from 4.2 to 5.8 percent of GDP, or more than a third. Income tax receipts grew from 7.6 percent to 9.2 percent of GDP between 1971 and 1981, an increase of 20 percent, despite a series of small tax cuts authorized by Congress. This reflected "bracket creep," the inflation of wages within a sharply progressive tax code. By the late 1970s popular discontent with taxes was widespread, and Republicans capitalized on this.

Ronald Reagan's landslide victory in the 1980 presidential election, which also gave the Republicans control of the U.S. Senate for the first time in twenty-five years, opened the way for change. His first action was among his most important. Immediately after his inauguration, Reagan ended all controls on domestically produced crude oil, in a stroke resolving a problem that had vexed his predecessor for four years. Other aspects of deregulation continued or expanded under Reagan. The administration also eased the enforcement of environmental and safety regulations. This process was clumsy, though, attuned more to saving business money than to balancing the costs and benefits of such regulations. The changes did reduce expenses for favored industries but did not resolve the basic problem in the area. Reagan also cut social spending by more than $40 billion. But his administration failed to reduce entitlements—benefits offered automatically to people in certain categories, like Medicare and Social Security—which consumed an ever-growing part of the federal budget. Indeed, the administration's first serious political defeat came when it tried to cut Social Security benefits for those who retired before the age of sixty-five. As a result, despite the initial reductions, social spending grew substantially during Reagan's tenure.

The Reagan administration had its greatest impact on the tax code. In 1981 it secured legislation reducing income tax rates 25 percent over three years and immediately cutting the top rate from 70 to 50 percent. Congress attached to this measure generous benefits for corporations, allowing greater deductions against taxes for investment outlays. By the mid-1980s income taxes were once again claiming 7.5 to 8 percent of GDP, the same level as in the 1960s, down from 9.2 percent in the late 1970s. A second wave of tax reform came in 1986, this time with support from many Democrats, including Senators Al Gore and Bill Bradley. Washington outlawed a host of tax shelters that had allowed many of the wealthy to avoid levies, increased the basic deduction to remove the poor from tax rolls, and cut the number of income tax brackets to three, ranging from 15 to 28 percent. Although designed to bring in as much money as the old system, with cuts in deductions financing lower rates, this measure in fact brought in more money, presumably because lower rates encouraged work or at least discouraged evasion, which was in any case more difficult. In 1986 income tax receipts totaled 7.9 percent of GDP; in 1989, under the new code, the total was 8.2 percent. It seems that, under the right conditions, reductions in tax rates could generate more revenue, though the effect was not nearly as dramatic as Laffer had predicted. During his administration, Reagan cut the top tax rate on individuals from 70 to 28 percent, with other rates down substantially as well—though not by 60 percent.

The benefits of these reductions did not accrue evenly. Overall the tax burden did not decline because Social Security levies rose substantially to fund the escalating costs of Medicare and old-age pensions. But Social Security taxes are a flat levy on income up to a certain point, so their increase did not substantially raise the marginal tax rate—the amount paid on each extra dollar of income. This was particularly true for those with high incomes. Provided they did not make too generous use of tax shelters before 1986, these people enjoyed a substantial reduction in levies, whereas most of the population only broke even.

Important as changes in taxes, spending, and regulation were for the long run, the Federal Reserve dominated the economic atmosphere in the first years of the Reagan administration. The transition from Carter to Reagan did not alter its policy. Paul Volcker remained in office, and he was determined to break inflation with high interest rates and slow monetary growth. Reagan backed him more strongly than had Carter. Although more famous for its supply-side initiatives, the Reagan administration viewed demand-side policies from a monetarist perspective. Volcker's program accorded with their own preferences. Carter's advisers had little use for such concepts, and they were less willing than their successors to accept higher unemployment as the price of stable prices.

The Fed's emphasis on monetary targets meant that interest rates fluctuated sharply, rising and falling inversely with the demand for credit. In late 1980 recession made individuals and business far less eager to take out loans, so monetary growth slowed and the Fed allowed interest rates to decline somewhat, which permitted the economy to rebound modestly. Revived economic activity in early 1981, however, brought new calls for loans and higher interest rates. By the fall of that year the prime rate exceeded 18 percent, by far the highest level in the twentieth century.

The extraordinary cost of money plunged the country back into recession. In 1982 housing starts fell to fewer than 1.1 million—the lowest level of the postwar era—and total investment fell by 14 percent. By the end of the year unemployment had surged to 11 percent, the worst since the depression. In states like Michigan and Ohio, which depended on heavy industry, conditions were worse. There, 15 percent or more of the workforce was unemployed. Between the end of 1979 and the end of 1982 the American economy did not grow at all, and some economists argued that the economy was sliding into another Great Depression.

Bad as conditions were, however, they did contain the basis for recovery. Although battered, the financial system continued to function—there was no panic. In the summer of 1982 the central bank relaxed its hold on credit, and money found its way to those who wanted it. The prime rate finally declined below 10 percent in 1983. The cost of money remained high by historical standards, but these reductions were nevertheless enough to permit a recovery. Investment increased by 9 percent in 1983 and 30 percent in 1984, fueling a strong expansion.

Several factors accounted for this change in Fed policy. First, the severity of the recession alarmed Volcker and his colleagues, who began to fear that they had pursued too extreme a course. And evidence strongly suggested that inflation was falling—the price of oil was actually lower, and wage increases had slowed substantially. Meanwhile the Fed's political support was evaporating. Even the Reagan administration, initially a supporter of tight money, was by 1982 questioning the wisdom of keeping rates up in the face of record unemployment.

However painful, the Federal Reserve's tight-money policy changed the long-term economic outlook for the better. It largely demolished expectations of inflation, which in the 1970s had forced prices higher even when the economy was weak. Consumer prices increased by little more than 3 percent in 1983, and recovery brought no acceleration in this rate. The experience largely validated Milton Friedman's analysis of the Phillips Curve, which suggested that a temporary increase in unemployment could bring a permanent drop in inflation—though Friedman probably had not realized just how large an increase in unemployment this would require. More broadly, the Federal Reserve had forced Americans to adjust their expectations to economic reality. Americans in the 1970s, taking the expansion of the 1950s and 1960s as their guide, had demanded advances in real wages and expansion of government programs that no longer accorded with the economy's capacity to produce. The terrible downturn of 1980–1982 made them willing to settle for less. The relative optimism of the 1980s did reflect better economic performance, but it also owed something to lower expectations.

Subsequently, attitudes toward inflation changed dramatically. Of course the Great Stagflation of the 1970s was not as bad as the Great Depression of the 1930s, but by 1980 more than half the population had been born after 1940 and so had no memory of the depression. The new generation would recoil instinctively from inflation the way their parents had from unemployment. Partly as a result, the central bank enjoyed much greater latitude to raise interest rates, if necessary, to contain prices.

BENEATH THE SURFACE

The Great Stagflation of 1973–1982 occurred because Americans demanded more of their economy than it could provide. Productivity, which had grown at about 3 percent a year since 1945, grew by less than 1 percent a year after 1973. In other words, behavior that before 1973 was consistent with stable prices—raises of 3 percent a year and comparable increases in private and government spending—became inflationary. The effect was cumulative. If workers who secured 3 percent raises discovered prices going up just as fast, they would demand 6 percent raises next time. When inflation ratcheted up to 6 percent, the next set of demands would be for raises of 9 percent.

Why did productivity stagnate? Some analysts argued that social changes in the 1960s eroded the work ethic, so that people did not labor as conscientiously, but there is no convincing evidence that average on-the-job diligence deteriorated. In fact the portion of the American population holding or actively seeking employment increased in the 1970s, from 60.4 percent to 63.8 percent—not the behavior of a people unwilling to work. Other analysts point to the oil crisis, emphasizing that higher productivity often requires the application of more energy. This is plausible, but it seems unlikely that an increase in the price of any single commodity, however important, would dislocate the American economy for an entire decade. Nor did the decline of oil prices in the 1980s unleash a sudden surge in productivity. Still others look to a drop in investment caused by inflation. Although the process of improving productivity is complex, it entails upgrading tools, organization, and worker skills, all of which require investment. Over time, inflation creates barriers to new investment by driving up long-term interest rates and decimating companies' depreciation reserves. But investment did not drop in the 1970s—indeed, in many years it made up a larger share of GDP than in the 1950s and 1960s.

Three other factors seem to have slowed productivity growth. First, the direction of investment apparently changed in the 1970s. Environmental regulations forced business to spend heavily on machinery to control pollution, and rising oil prices encouraged investment in conservation. In essence, much of capital spending went to lower the cost of energy and protect the environment, not to make people more efficient. Less important but also a factor, oil companies invested huge amounts to get crude out of inhospitable places like the North Slope of Alaska and the North Sea of the Atlantic.

Changes in the labor market further retarded productivity growth. Between 1965 and 1985 the workforce increased by 55 percent, to almost 115 million. Over the previous twenty years, 1945 to 1965, the increase had been only 38 percent. Three developments accounted for this increase. First, the baby boom generation came to maturity. Second, more women entered the workforce, availing themselves of greater opportunities created by new legislation and evolving social attitudes. At the same time stagnant wages led many housewives who might not otherwise have done so to take jobs to preserve and expand family income. Third, changes in immigration laws in the 1960s allowed more foreign workers into the country, a development that would have even greater impact in the 1980s and 1990s.

The growing labor force created several difficulties. Throughout the 1945–1973 period American workers were highly productive because industry supported them with expensive training, tools, and organization. A substantial increase in employment required heavy investment simply to make new work-ers as efficient as the old. The existence of a large pool of workers also gave employers less incentive to increase productivity. Com-panies could meet higher demand by hiring new people rather than by increasing the output of existing employees, a tendency reinforced as environmental regulations and rising oil prices re-quired capital spending in those areas.

Perhaps most important in the long run, many of the tech-niques used by American firms to improve productivity had by the 1970s apparently reached the point of diminishing returns. For most of the twentieth century U.S. companies had empha-sized mass production. The auto plant was the ultimate example of this, with thousands of workers on an assembly line, each using machines designed for a specific task ("dedicated") to per-form over and over again one small part of assembling a car. The result was a huge number of identical, inexpensive, and fairly re-liable automobiles. Other industries, from fast food to construc-tion, had applied this model to their own needs. Americans had achieved extraordinary things with mass production, creating a standard of living unimaginable a century earlier. But every technique has its limits, and by the 1970s the United States may well have extracted as much benefit from this one as possible. Further advances would require moving beyond mass produc-tion.

4

Adjusting to New Realities

IN THE 1980s the American economy presented a mixed picture. Many statistics suggested that, after 1982, the United States enjoyed remarkable prosperity, but other figures indicated a growing inequality of wealth and income and weakness in critical sectors. Observers often used whatever data supported their intellectual convictions and political self-interests. Few generalizations, however, adequately described the evolution of the country's economy. In the 1970s American industry had developed serious structural problems reflected in stagnant productivity and income. Inflation had partially concealed these. Yet rising prices worked on structural problems like morphine on a broken limb: the pain abated but the injury persisted—and the painkiller itself might create new problems. After 1982 the United States had to confront structural weakness and cope with the aftermath of inflation—that is, repair the system while withdrawing from the painkiller.

THE DUAL ECONOMY

In aggregate terms the American economy performed well between 1983 and 1989. Gross Domestic Product grew, on average, almost 4 percent a year, and consumer prices advanced at about 3.5 percent annually. Unemployment fell from 11 percent at the start of 1983 to less than 5.5 percent in 1989, even though the labor force grew by 12 percent over the same period.

Other statistics suggested a less optimistic assessment. Productivity (output per hour worked) improved only slightly more rapidly after 1982 than in the preceding decade. Without higher productivity, real (inflation-adjusted) wages could not increase. During the long 1983–1989 boom Americans enjoyed predictable prices and expanding job opportunities, but their income grew little. And the benefits of prosperity accrued unevenly; differences between both classes and regions increased substantially.

The gap between rich and poor widened. In the decades after World War II the distribution of income in the United States was fairly stable, but the situation changed in the late 1970s. In 1977 the poorest 20 percent of American families received 4.4 percent of national income; by 1993 their share had dropped to 3.6 percent. Because overall income grew only slowly, this meant that the real earnings of the poorest section of society actually declined somewhat—a major hardship for people already struggling. Meanwhile the wealthiest 20 percent of families increased their share of total income from 43.6 to 48.9 percent.

Why did this happen? Democrats blamed the Reagan administration, which reduced both taxes on the wealthy and social programs for the poor. Figures on income distribution, however, take neither taxes nor government benefits into account. The Reagan administration did weaken government policies that redistributed income from rich to poor, but this cannot account for the growth of underlying inequality. Social developments played a major role. In the 1970s and 1980s single-parent households became more common. Because such families have only one adult to care for children and earn money, they usually have lower incomes than two-parent households. At the other end of the economic spectrum, more well-educated women continued to work after getting married, a major change from the 1950s and 1960s. Because their spouses also tended to be well educated, such couples enjoyed particularly high incomes.

Changes in the economic structure were at least as important. The decline of heavy industry reduced the number of high-paying jobs for semi-skilled workers while the rapid growth of the information technology sector allowed those with appropriate education and training to command premium wages. The minimum wage also remained unchanged for almost a decade after 1982 despite rising prices, largely because the Reagan administration opposed meddling in the free market.

Some factors mitigated growing inequality. As had always been the case in the United States, individuals moved between income groups. Many in the bottom 20 percent were young people just starting in life who would ultimately improve their position. Many in the top group were at the peak of their careers and would, upon retirement, fall back somewhat. A growing portion of those at the bottom were immigrants who, whatever their relative position in the United States, were earning far more than they could in their home countries. Nevertheless any development that made life harder for society's least fortunate was reason for concern.

Substantial regional differences also emerged in the period. Such disparities were not new—some areas of the country have always been wealthier than others. For instance, income in the South has been well below the national average for generations. Still, the economies of the various parts of the United States have usually expanded or contracted in unison. Such was not the case in the 1980s. Heavy industry (steel, automobiles, machinery), concentrated in the Midwest, recovered only slowly from the 1980–1982 recession, largely because of intense foreign competition. Commodity-producing regions—the "oil patch" and "farm belt"—fared worse. High commodity prices in the early 1970s had led producers to expand output and consumers to limit purchases. The case of oil is instructive. High petroleum prices encouraged conservation, and by 1985 the United States secured 25 percent more output for each unit of energy than it had done a decade earlier. Meanwhile new oil fields in Alaska, the North Sea, and Mexico began producing on a large scale. By 1980 petroleum shortages had largely disappeared, but inflation and the operation of OPEC temporarily concealed shifting market conditions, keeping prices high. A collapse was inevitable. Between 1980 and 1986 oil prices declined from almost $40 a barrel to little more than $10 a barrel. OPEC found itself unable to control its members, who cut prices below the officially sanctioned level to sell their oil in a glutted market. The markets for other commodities, like copper and wheat, followed a similar pattern: shortages in the early 1970s, greater production and conservation in the late 1970s, and rapid price declines in the 1980s. Falling prices set off a cascade of bankruptcies among American drillers, miners, farmers, and their creditors—farm foreclosures reached levels not seen since the Great Depression of the 1930s. In 1985 a visitor to Houston or to one of the country's many farming communities would have found not signs of prosperity but rather abandoned homes, empty office buildings, and boarded-up storefronts.

Yet growing inequality between classes and regions sparked no great political upheaval. Populist figures such as Senator Tom Harkin won elections in places like Iowa, hard hit by falling agricultural prices, but he and figures like him had limited national impact. Several factors account for this relative complacency. The Reagan administration proved in some cases more flexible than its free-market rhetoric suggested. It spent huge amounts on farm programs, funneling money through structures whose origins lay in the New Deal; it rescued banks hurt by the collapse of oil prices; and it persuaded the Japanese to limit auto exports to the United States, giving American car producers a respite from competition. Such measures did not resolve the problems of depressed sectors, but they mitigated difficulties and demonstrated government concern.

More important, there were genuine reasons for optimism. Even as basic industries struggled to survive and regions dependent on commodities suffered recession, new sectors enjoyed spectacular growth. Their expansion was sufficient to keep the larger economy growing and to absorb most of the workers who lost jobs elsewhere.

Information technology led the way. With the important exception of consumer electronics, U.S. companies were in the forefront of every sector of this diverse industry. Cable television represented an early and lasting success. This technology had existed as long as television itself, but government policy had limited cable service to areas that over-the-air stations did not reach. But in the 1970s Congress gradually relaxed these regulations, and by 1980 control had effectively ceased. The result was an extraordinary boom. Between 1980 and 1990 the number of homes with cable television increased from eight million to forty million. This huge investment not only stimulated the manufacture of cable, switching gear, and the like but also created a permanent demand for programming on a scale previously unimaginable. In the early 1970s Time Inc. had founded the first cable network, Home Box Office (HBO), to show movies, and many others soon followed its lead. These organizations soon discovered that rerunning old movies and television series developed for the three broadcast networks would not hold viewers. They had to develop their own shows. Television studios' production expanded accordingly, and much of this programming eventually found its way abroad, either sold to networks in other countries or shown by the foreign subsidiaries of U.S. cable networks.

Computers demonstrated even more dramatic growth. The

development of the microprocessor by Intel and Texas Instruments in the late 1960s had inaugurated a period of rapid advance in the power of computers. Producers were able, on average, to double the power of these chips every eighteen months—a pace unmatched in the history of any other technology. More powerful microprocessors allowed more powerful, less expensive computers. By the mid-1970s several firms had introduced microcomputers, which fit on a desk and were within the means of individuals. The first machines were not very powerful and sold chiefly to hobbyists, but by 1980 Apple Computer and several other firms had developed reliable microcomputers that ran a variety of useful programs.

IBM revolutionized the field in 1981 by introducing the Personal Computer (PC). By any definition IBM was the leader in the computer field, and simply by offering the PC it encouraged many producers and consumers who had thought of microcomputers as toys now to take them seriously. By 1984 IBM was selling three million PCs a year. The IBM PC instantly became the industry standard for which other firms wrote software and offered peripheral devices such as modems. By 1985 only Apple with its Macintosh used a different architecture. But the profits from IBM's achievement largely went to others. To guarantee that its product became the industry standard, IBM freely licensed its technology. This allowed firms like Dell, Compaq, and Gateway to offer PC "clones" at prices below IBM's. More important, the central components of clones were microprocessors and operating software, which came from Intel and Microsoft, respectively—not IBM. Profit margins on these items were high—far higher than on PCs themselves—and Intel and Microsoft eventually became two of the world's more profitable companies.

Despite IBM's missteps—or perhaps because of them—the industry developed fast. Throughout the 1980s the power of PCs mushroomed as their cost fell. In 1984 Apple introduced the first operating system using icons and a mouse, and Microsoft issued a roughly comparable system for PCs—Windows—the following year. By 1990 computers were ubiquitous in American life.

Genetic engineering seemed to offer opportunities almost as great as information technology. In the 1980s scientific advances opened up the possibility of altering the very structure of living organisms, allowing the creation of drugs that treated serious diseases without side effects and of crops naturally immune to various pests. A variety of small companies with promising ideas managed to attract large investments, but progress was slow. By the 1990s the first products of genetic engineering—drugs and seeds—appeared on the market, but the industry was still far from repaying the large sums invested in it.

By the 1980s over three-quarters of the American economy consisted of services, and overall growth reflected steady expansion in that sector. In many cases the development of this sector followed long-established trends. The percentage of young people who finished college, 31 percent in 1970, climbed to more than 40 percent by the end of the century. Health-care outlays continued to grow despite efforts by government and private insurers to limit them. Financial services expanded, following a trend evident since the late 1940s. As the population aged, the demand for nursing homes increased; as the number of working mothers grew, so did demand for day-care.

Innovations did occur, however. New developments in retailing and manufacturing required precisely scheduled deliveries, providing new opportunities for shippers. Cable systems required a constant stream of new programming. Computers involved data processing and software. The products of genetic engineering needed extensive testing. Another trend, unrelated to technology, also provided new opportunities. More firms subcontracted for services like cleaning and security, which had traditionally been performed in-house. Specialized firms enjoyed economies of scale and a breadth of experience unavailable to any in-house operation, and the results were often higher quality at lower cost. At the least, corporate officers no longer had to worry about the cleaning staff.

Most Americans recognized that economic conditions after 1982 were not ideal, but they also realized that the situation was far better than in the preceding decade. In particular they benefited from stable inflation and demonstrated little tolerance for measures that might push prices higher. Unwilling to go back, they accepted change, putting on it the best aspect possible. This attitude helps explain Ronald Reagan's landslide reelection in 1984 as well as the elevation of his vice president, George Bush, to the presidency in 1988.

Laissez Faire?

Although most famous for cutting taxes, the Reagan administration altered anti-trust and labor policy in ways that would affect the structure of the U.S. economy into the next century. These initiatives effectively eliminated barriers to change, facilitating the reorganization of American industry. The essence of Reaganism was to give private enterprise as much leeway and as many resources as possible on the assumption that, in a free market, companies would make the best decisions for their own and thus for the country's economic well-being.

Reform of anti-trust represented the culmination of long intellectual ferment. The anti-trust statutes are notoriously vague, varying considerably depending on who interprets them. After 1945 a strict interpretation of these measures predominated. Most notably, the courts largely banned mergers between firms in the same or related fields. In the 1970s, however, a group of scholars centered at the University of Chicago suggested a new approach to anti-trust that became known as the "law and economics movement." They argued that consumer welfare was the proper object of the anti-trust laws and that courts should employ economic analysis to decide cases. For instance, if the structure of an industry was such that outsiders could easily enter it or that numerous substitutes existed for its products, then the merger of companies within that industry offered little reason for concern. No combination, no matter how large, could raise prices for long without attracting competition that would force them back down. To this point the logic of law and economics was hard to deny. Advocates of this approach took the matter further, however. Most were enthusiasts of the free market who believed that monopoly and market power were extremely rare. Companies that exploited temporary positions of strength to raise prices would, they believed, inevitably attract competition that would force prices back into line. Exceptions did exist, but more often than not they rested on some sort of government favoritism. Essentially law and economics reversed the presumption against mergers that had guided the law for a generation, implying a major relaxation of anti-trust enforcement.

Reagan's Justice Department embraced law and economics. It dropped an anti-trust suit against IBM and settled one against AT&T on terms that the company favored while still opening the long-distance telephone market to competition. Mergers between firms in related fields and even between direct competitors became much easier. For instance, between 1980 and 2000 Gulf, Texaco, and Chevron joined together, as did Mobil and Exxon, consolidating the nation's five largest oil producers into two firms. This new attitude toward anti-trust endured beyond the Reagan administration—Exxon and Mobil merged during the presidency of Democrat Bill Clinton.

Whereas changes in anti-trust policy represented the culmination of a deliberate process, new labor policies evolved piecemeal.

ing labor relations. Some companies moved operations from the Northeast and Midwest to locations in the South and the West, where unions were relatively weak. In other cases, unionized firms subcontracted tasks once performed in-house to nonunion firms.

Some unions did adapt to new conditions. The United Auto Workers (UAW), traditionally one of the nation's strongest unions, acquiesced to a sharp reduction in employment and radical changes in work rules at General Motors, Ford, and Chrysler in exchange for the preservation of high wages and generous benefits. Indeed, there is little doubt that firms that negotiated needed changes with their unions did better than those that resorted, by choice or necessity, to confrontation. American Airlines navigated deregulation so well in part because it secured major changes in work rules from its unions without strikes. But however prudent, concessions led workers to doubt the utility of unions. The inability of the UAW to preserve jobs at the American auto companies may explain why it failed to organize plants built in the United States in the 1980s by Japanese firms— Honda, Toyota, and Nissan. Unions faced unappetizing options. They could make concessions, preserving a role for themselves but losing much of their credibility with members, or they could resist, risking strikes that might well destroy either themselves or the companies for which their members worked.

Organized labor suffered most, perhaps, from the changing structure of the American economy. Outside transportation and some utilities, unions were rare among service workers, but in the 1980s services accounted for the entire net increase in employment. Organized labor also played little role in information technology, the economy's most dynamic sector.

All these factors created a precipitous decline in the role of organized labor. As late as 1970 organized labor represented a third of the nonagricultural workforce. By 1990 the number was down to 16 percent, and it continued to fall. Increasingly, organized labor concentrated on those working in government, who did not have to worry about competition, domestic or foreign. By the 1990s fewer than 10 percent of workers in the private sector belonged to unions—roughly the same portion as in 1930.

Only dramatic political action could have arrested this trend. Legislation preventing employers from laying off or replacing workers, reimposing regulations on transportation, and limiting imports that competed with American products might well have allowed unions to maintain their position. But the Reagan administration had no intention of doing any of these things, all of which ran against its commitment to reduce restrictions on business. Legislation drastic enough to preserve organized labor would have imposed heavy costs on the rest of society, raising expenses across the board and quite likely reducing employment prospects. The case of continental Europe is instructive. Laws there made it difficult to discharge workers or eliminate an established union, and in the 1980s organized labor suffered far less deterioration of membership and power in Europe than in the United States. But by making it difficult to dismiss workers, such laws made companies extremely cautious about hiring, effectively limiting employment. Unemployment in most of Western Europe failed to decline much below 10 percent during the 1980s and 1990s. In contrast, greater liberty to dismiss workers made American companies more willing to hire. Unemployment in the United States exceeded 10 percent in only one year, 1982, and during large parts of the 1980s and 1990s the country reached full employment.

Could the United States have achieved the same end without eviscerating unions? Certainly some companies did negotiate new arrangements with organized labor, securing needed changes while preserving a role for unions. But confrontation is central to the American tradition of labor relations. In the view of most of their leaders, unions existed to protect workers from management, and these people were reluctant to accept contracts that reduced members' job prospects and improved employers' earnings, even if the long-term survival of companies—and therefore of members' jobs—depended on it. Even if union leadership did negotiate such agreements, the membership might not accept them. For its part, management often eagerly seized the opportunity to cripple unions without seriously exploring opportunities for compromise. A different outcome was possible but unlikely.

THE TWIN DEFICITS

During the 1980s the budget and trade deficits dominated public discussion of economic policy. Unlike questions of income inequality, union membership, anti-trust law, or depressed industries, they served as a convenient focus for concerns about the future widely shared by Americans. The budget deficit raised questions about the ability of the federal government to deal decisively with national problems, and the trade deficit raised doubts about the country's ability to maintain its position in the world.

Total federal debt grew more rapidly in the 1980s than at any time since World War II. During the 1980–1982 recession the deficit expanded sharply as revenue fell and Washington spent freely on unemployment insurance and other relief measures. But the scale of federal borrowing, in terms of percent of GDP, was roughly comparable to that during the 1973–1975 recession, and most economists consider deficits accrued during a recession inevitable and even beneficial. Deficits became a real problem only after 1982. Economic recovery brought no drop in federal borrowing, which remained in the vicinity of $150 to $200 billion a year, or roughly 3 to 5 percent of GDP, for the rest of the decade. Between 1980 and 1996 total government debt as a portion of GDP doubled, from one-third of GDP to two-thirds. Over the same period Washington's annual interest expenses grew from 1.9 percent of GDP to 3.2 percent, or by 68 percent.

Why did deficits remain so high when the overall economy was prosperous? Democrats blamed President Reagan's tax cuts and defense buildup, pointing out that between 1980 and 1986, in terms of percent of GDP, income tax revenue fell by almost 20 percent and military outlays grew by 30 percent. This led to an increase in the deficit equal to about 3 percent of GDP. The administration's reductions in domestic spending did not come close to paying for this charge. Republicans, taking a longer perspective, blamed deficits on growing social outlays. They observed that taxes, as a portion of GDP, were slightly higher in 1985 than in 1965, whereas defense spending was slightly lower. Nevertheless in 1965 the federal deficit was negligible, whereas in 1985 it was huge. Outlays for Social Security, Medicare, and Medicaid accounted for almost all the difference. Federal health-care outlays grew from .25 percent of GDP in 1965 to 2.4 percent two decades later (860 percent), and old-age pensions from 2.4 to 4.5 percent of GDP over the same period (84 percent).

Although the factors cited by both Republicans and Democrats were certainly important, at its core the deficit reflected anemic growth in productivity and income after 1973. In the 1970s federal revenue grew by 36 percent in real (inflation-adjusted) terms, and in the 1980s growth was 29 percent. By contrast, in the 1950s the jump was more than 84 percent, and in the 1960s it was 59 percent despite Kennedy's tax cut. Ultimately government revenue depends on national income. Had income grown as fast between 1970 and 1990 as between 1950 and 1970, revenue probably would have been sufficient to fund all of Washington's obligations. During the 1970s inflation concealed the extent of the problem, as it did many other economic weaknesses. Bracket creep automatically increased the effective rate of taxes, and rising prices cut into real (inflation-adjusted) government expenses and debt. Even programs indexed to inflation, like Social Security, raised outlays only a year after prices had jumped. Stable inflation, coupled with a new tax structure that largely undid the effects of bracket creep, made the government's uncomfortable financial position obvious.

Did large deficits matter? Certainly some of the rhetoric on the issue was apocalyptic. Commentators bemoaned the burden that the growing federal debt would impose on the nation's children and grandchildren and offered dire predictions of the tax increases and spending cuts required to service this huge and growing obligation. In the short run, however, the results were not so alarming. The economy did fairly well during the era of deficits. Between 1983 and 1996, when the deficit began to contract substantially, the country suffered only one recession, the relatively mild downturn of 1990–1991. Inflation, which is traditionally associated with heavy government borrowing, was stable throughout the period.

Nevertheless federal deficits created serious difficulties in two areas. First, they weakened the financial position of the federal government. By sharply increasing Washington's debt burden and its reliance on borrowing, the deficits made it hard for the government to respond aggressively to new circumstances that demanded spending. Washington was unable to adopt stimulative measures during the 1990–1991 recession, and it had to rely on its allies to pay for the 1991 Gulf War. Foreign lenders financed much of the government's borrowing, raising the prospect that a financial crisis abroad might suddenly cut off access to needed credit. The larger the debt became, the greater these problems. In practice, financial weakness did the United

States little harm, but this reflected good luck and clever management. In the long run, neither is a substitute for financial strength.

Second, government deficits kept interest rates much higher than they would have been otherwise. During the 1980s the prime rate never fell under 8 percent, and the rate on the bonds of the most creditworthy companies never declined below 9 percent. Considering that inflation hovered between 3 and 4 percent, the cost of money remained extraordinarily high. This reflected the need of the central bank to provide for government deficits without expanding the money supply dramatically. Although it had abandoned explicit targets for monetary growth in 1982, the Fed still took account of monetary growth and remained vigilant against inflation. High rates limited private borrowing and attracted money from abroad, allowing Washington to finance its debt without expanding the money supply in an inflationary fashion. In a sense, then, Americans paid for deficits not in higher taxes but in higher interest rates.

High interest rates had two negative consequences. First, they made investment more expensive. Of course, lower taxes did leave firms and individuals with more money to invest, but it is not clear that this fully compensated for the higher cost of borrowing. Capital spending as a portion of GDP was slightly lower in the 1980s than in the 1970s, though a little stronger than in the 1950s and 1960s. Home buyers in particular suffered. Interest rates have a huge impact on the size of mortgage payments, and because of the high cost of money, home buyers in the 1980s had either to make larger payments or to settle for less desirable homes than in earlier years. Second, high interest rates led to an extraordinary appreciation of the dollar. Foreigners purchased greenbacks to invest at the high interest rates offered in the United States, and between 1980 and 1985 these purchases drove the dollar up more than 60 percent against the currencies of the

other industrial democracies. Such rapid appreciation created serious problems for American firms competing against foreign rivals. The federal deficit was therefore related to the other deficit
that attracted public attention during the 1980s—the trade
deficit.

During the 1980s the United States ran a huge deficit on its
current account. Unlike the federal deficit, this gap grew rather
than diminished in the 1990s. In 1980 the current account had
been in balance, with a surplus on services and investment income compensating for a small trade deficit. In fact trade was expanding fast, with exports growing from 3.7 percent of GDP in
1969 to 8.1 percent in 1980. This reflected strong demand for
U.S. farm commodities, large devaluations of the dollar in
1971–1973 and 1977–1979, and the somewhat belated realization
by American companies that foreign markets, particularly in Europe, were often as rich as the domestic one. Of course, imports
grew apace. Oil was the largest single factor, but foreign steel,
consumer electronics, and automobiles made significant inroads
into U.S. markets. Still, from an aggregate point of view, the situation was favorable.

The rapid appreciation of the dollar changed things. It priced
many American goods out of foreign markets, and between 1980
and 1985, exports slipped from 8.1 to 5.1 percent of GDP while
imports remained stable as a portion of GDP. Services and investment income remained in surplus (barely), but they were not
nearly enough to compensate for the trade deficit. By 1986 the
overall deficit on the U.S. current account was more than $100
billion. By the end of the decade the United States had, for the
first time since World War I, become a net debtor on its international account, owing the rest of the world, in aggregate, more
than it was owed.

Exports began to recover after 1985. The industrial democracies launched a concerted effort to drive down the price of the

dollar, and currency markets responded—traders had apparently concluded that the dollar could not remain so high indefinitely. The dollar fell by more than a third between 1985 and 1988, and exports rebounded to 6.7 percent of GDP by 1990. But although encouraging, the growth of exports was not enough to erase the trade deficit.

The U.S. government also redoubled efforts to open foreign markets to American products. Although the Reagan administration protected favored domestic industries like automobiles, it retained a strong ideological commitment to free trade. Trade is one of the issues on which almost all economists agree. Countries, they argue, should concentrate on products they make most efficiently, exporting them in exchange for goods and services in whose production they are less adept. This will allow the highest level of output and living standards worldwide. The Reagan administration, like almost every administration since World War II, accepted this analysis. Self-interest also figured into the administration's preference. Contrary to popular perception, the United States did not practice completely free trade. Imports often faced restrictions that put foreign sellers at a disadvantage and, in a few cases like textiles, could be prohibitive. Nevertheless the American market was more open than those of most other industrial countries—particularly Japan, which ran a huge surplus with the United States. This observation led to the conclusion that the elimination of trade barriers would benefit American exporters disproportionately. In 1984 the Reagan administration signed an agreement with Canada eliminating almost all restrictions on trade between the two countries and harmonizing many regulations that affected imports. This represented the first of a series of regional and worldwide agreements designed to reduce trade barriers. Like the accord with Canada, these agreements addressed not only tariffs and import quotas but also regulations that, though not ostensibly related to trade, could put foreign sellers at a disadvantage.

In the 1980s many Americans feared that the growing trade deficit reflected a decline in the "competitiveness" of U.S. industry. Citing the success of foreign—particularly Japanese—firms in the American market, they warned that the country had entered a period of industrial decline. In many ways the discussion missed the point. Economic competition occurs between firms, not countries. Inevitably some companies do well against foreign rivals and some do not. Moreover, any dynamic economy's industrial composition is constantly changing, so that the decline of one industry or group of industries does not necessarily portend general decline. Yet defined narrowly, this discussion did highlight some serious problems with the U.S. economy.

As a practical matter, the question of deteriorating competitiveness affected only a few sectors. In aerospace, computers, chemicals, pharmaceuticals, and telecommunications equipment, the United States consistently exported more than it imported. U.S. firms making consumer products—soap, chocolate, condiments, and the like—did equally well, though they usually operated abroad through foreign subsidiaries rather than exports. After the mid-1970s the United States also consistently enjoyed a surplus on services. The increase in the dollar's value after 1980 did hurt companies in all these areas, but they rebounded quickly after 1985 as the greenback returned to more appropriate levels. Labor-intensive industries like shoes, textiles, and apparel did lose ground permanently to foreign competition, but this was probably inevitable. These sectors have low productivity and rarely pay workers much more than the minimum wage. A dynamic economy should constantly be moving people from such industries into others in which productivity and wages are higher. The process is wrenching for those involved, but it is necessary for the ongoing improvement of living standards.

American firms, however, also lost ground in several capital-intensive industries that paid high wages, such as steel, automobiles, machine tools, and consumer electronics. This was genuine cause for alarm. Cheaper foreign labor and the high dollar could not explain the problem; aerospace, aluminum, and chemical firms remained competitive in a roughly comparable environment. Rather, in the troubled fields foreign companies were producing higher-quality goods more efficiently than their American rivals.

Each industry had its own story. In steel, problems dated from the 1950s, when American producers failed to invest in the new basic oxygen and continuous-casting technologies. Even when competition forced U.S. producers to invest in these technologies in the 1970s and 1980s, they did so only gradually and only by installing new equipment in old plants, which made it difficult to realize the full productivity gains that green-field plants using these techniques would have offered. Established steel producers also overlooked another technology that allowed small domestic firms to challenge them: electric furnaces. "Minimills" used electric furnaces to turn scrap metal into steel, and unlike open hearth or basic oxygen furnaces, they were efficient at a relatively small size. Entrepreneurs generally located these plants in the South, where they enjoyed cheaper, nonunion labor.

The major American steel producers responded to the foreign challenge by seeking government protection. They asked for relief under the anti-dumping statutes, which banned foreign firms from selling in the United States for prices below those they charged at home. This strategy enjoyed some success, but it did nothing to erase the basic weakness of U.S. companies. The United States had fallen from the rank of first to third among the world's steel producers, behind China and Japan. U.S. Steel, which had once made more steel than any entire country other than the United States, only barely retained a position among the world's ten largest steel firms.

Different industries developed differently. The American consumer electronics industry collapsed under foreign pressure.

By 1990 the United States relied on Japanese companies like Sony for new products such as CD, VCR, and DVD players. In contrast the automobile industry cut costs, improved quality, and introduced lucrative new products like minivans and sport utility vehicles (SUVs). The quality of its vehicles still fell short of the very best offered by the Japanese, who continued to account for a large share of the American market, but U.S. firms remained viable competitors. In the late 1980s the United States reclaimed from Japan the position of the world's largest producer of automobiles, which it had lost earlier in the decade—although unlike Japan, the United States exported little of its production, and the American figures included the output of Japanese-owned plants in the United States.

However different were subsequent developments, problems usually had the same origin. American companies, having made themselves world leaders in the 1940s and 1950s, became complacent and failed to continue to upgrade their products and production. Foreign competitors did not stand still, and by the 1970s they had caught up with and even surpassed their U.S. rivals. Devaluation of the dollar in 1971–1973 and 1977–1978 delayed the reckoning by giving American firms a temporary cost advantage against foreign rivals, but it did not resolve the basic problem. Stabilization in the early 1980s—the decline of inflation and the increase in the dollar's value—forced producers to adjust or go out of business.

Despite these issues—or perhaps because of them—American manufacturing enjoyed a renaissance of sorts beginning in the mid-1980s. Overall, productivity in the sector advanced about 3 percent a year after 1982. Better productivity owed much to the pressures and example of foreign competition. Japanese and European firms selling in the United States increasingly built plants here. These new factories were invariably state-of-the-art, and they usually performed as well as the foreign owner's home facilities. They upgraded U.S. manufacturing capability and provided an example for their American-based rivals to emulate.

In particular, American companies borrowed two techniques from the Japanese. The first was just-in-time inventories, pioneered by Toyota. Traditionally manufacturers had kept large inventories of raw materials and parts to guarantee that a shortage anywhere along the assembly line would not disrupt production. But these inventories were expensive, and they required warehousing and cataloguing. Starting in the 1950s Toyota developed a system that delivered parts along the line only as needed. This not only eliminated the considerable expenses associated with inventories but also better coordinated the whole assembly process, forcing each operation to adjust to the overall pace of production. By the 1990s just-in-time inventories had become standard practice in American plants.

The other major adoption, "total quality control," actually originated with an American, W. Edwards Deming. In the 1940s Deming had developed a statistical system to identify the origins of product defects—in other words, what had gone wrong in the first place. After World War II American firms had largely ignored Deming's ideas, instead inspecting final products and fixing those that did not work properly. But this labor-intensive process did not address the causes of defects. The Japanese, in contrast, adopted Deming's approach wholeheartedly—one of the top awards in Japanese industry bears Deming's name. Total quality control, by locating the causes of defects and so preventing them from recurring, not only improved quality but also saved the large sums spent repairing faulty products. Ideally Deming's system integrated workers closely into the process, giving them responsibility for identifying and correcting defects on the assembly line. The American tradition of confrontation in labor relations made it hard to adopt Deming's program *in toto,* but by 1990 most U.S. manufacturers had adopted some form of total quality control.

REORGANIZATION

The revival of American industry required more than efficient production techniques. In the United States, as in every developed country, corporate infrastructure consumed as much or more resources than production. Marketing, distribution, design, purchasing, research, and accounting must be uniformly efficient for a company to succeed. By the late 1970s many U.S. companies were not performing these tasks as well as they might. The problem was not so much that they had fallen behind foreign competitors; rather, companies had become bloated and unfocused. The growth of corporate bureaucracy represented the most obvious aspect of this phenomenon. In 1980 at Ford, for example, seventeen layers of bureaucracy stood between the average worker and the company's president. This not only represented a substantial cost but actually inhibited effective management. During the 1970s accelerating inflation allowed firms to stay ahead of rising costs—indeed, inflation often made it difficult to know exactly what expenses were. Nevertheless by the end of the decade profits in many sectors were deteriorating. The 1980–1982 recession forced adjustment.

In the 1980s and early 1990s companies focused on reducing costs. They reviewed their organization and installations and got rid of what they did not need. In practice this meant dismissing employees—advocates euphemistically described the process as "downsizing." Between 1979 and 1983 Ford Motor Company shrank from 500,000 employees to 380,000; over the same period Firestone Tire dismissed 24,000, or 22 percent of its workforce. The process continued into the next decade. In 1993 and 1994

IBM dismissed 60,000 employees. Downsizing was particularly brutal in companies facing sharp foreign competition; they not only had to cut costs but adjust to a smaller share of the total market.

Downsizing had sweeping social implications. In the post–World War II era, managers at large companies had enjoyed considerable job security. Barring dishonesty, gross incompetence, or exceptional bad luck, they had jobs for life. Such people were foremost among the casualties of downsizing as firms closed entire offices or even divisions. For the first time since the Great Depression, unemployment seriously affected the middle class. The change was scarcely less traumatic for low-level workers. Although often laid off during recessions, before 1980 they had almost always been able to return to their old jobs when conditions improved. During the 1980s and early 1990s, however, many plants closed permanently, forcing workers to find new jobs. In particular, union members from steel and auto plants rarely found new positions that paid as well as the old. The closure of plants and offices also devastated communities whose economies depended on these installations—the populations of many industrial cities actually declined in the 1980s.

Although usually necessary, downsizing posed risks to companies. Managers might, in their enthusiasm to reduce expenses, weaken or eliminate vital functions. Mass firings inevitably devastated employee morale. Perhaps most important, downsizing was not in and of itself a formula for success. Profitable companies produce goods or services that consumers want. Efficiently providing something no one desires will still yield bankruptcy. Downsizing worked at Ford because the company simultaneously improved the quality of its goods and developed appealing new products like the Taurus sedan and the Explorer SUV. It failed at Sunbeam because the firm continued to offer the same tired line of appliances that did not interest consumers.

Still, on balance downsizing strengthened companies and the American economy. Many of the firms that executed such programs would not otherwise have survived. More broadly, downsizing increased both productivity and profits. By dismissing superfluous employees, companies improved the per capita output of the remainder. Lower costs also improved corporate profits, which ultimately finance all investment. In the long run, higher productivity translated into better wages, and greater profits into more capital spending. Although it may seem perverse, a country can indeed downsize its way to prosperity.

Companies not only cut expenses but also refined their focus, a process that continued through the end of the century. Although the vogue for conglomerates faded in the 1970s, companies still often diversified into unrelated fields—Exxon began selling office machinery, U.S. Steel purchased an oil company, and Coca-Cola invested in a movie studio. By the 1980s, however, opinion had turned decisively against such policies. The authors of *In Pursuit of Excellence,* a best-selling 1982 book on management, advised companies to "stick to your knitting" and warned that diversification made sense only if it rested on established capabilities. Firms increasingly followed this advice. They sold off divisions unrelated to their core operations and used the proceeds to strengthen their main lines of business, often through acquisitions and mergers. The result was the growth of ever-larger companies focused on specific industries. Consumer products companies such as Philip Morris expanded their portfolio of consumer brands, in Philip Morris's case by purchasing Kraft Foods and General Foods. Between 1980 and 2000 the country's five largest oil companies coalesced into two firms, and Alcoa absorbed Reynolds aluminum, its chief rival. By the end of the century the nation's railroads had come together in four large systems. In all these cases, companies sought economies of scale and scope in their core business. Consumer products firms sold more brands of goods through their existing marketing organizations. Aluminum and petroleum firms concentrated output in the largest, most efficient plants, closing less productive ones. Larger railroad systems could better coordinate through traffic. The more permissive attitude toward anti-trust enforcement in the 1980s and 1990s was critical to the success of these mergers, which in most cases probably would not have passed legal scrutiny in the 1950s and 1960s.

Corporate reorganization also allowed companies to change their focus in line with new economic realities. The chemical and petroleum industries offer perhaps the best example. In the 1980s and early 1990s firms like DuPont and Monsanto sold most of their petrochemical divisions to oil companies. Although these businesses had once been quite profitable, the increase of oil prices in the 1970s had badly hurt them, and by the 1980s petrochemicals had become a fiercely competitive industry with low profit margins. The oil companies had more experience managing large-volume, low-margin businesses, and they could, by integrating petrochemicals into their refining operations, achieve economies unavailable to chemical firms. Moreover, receipts from petrochemicals reduced oil firms' dependence on the sale of gasoline and heating oil, whose price was volatile. Chemical firms took the proceeds from the sale of their petrochemical divisions and invested in new areas promising higher profits: pharmaceuticals, genetic engineering, and agricultural chemicals.

Of course, the success of corporate reorganization was not automatic. After losing its telephone monopoly in 1984, AT&T reorganized itself several times, buying and selling off computer, cellular phone, and cable television companies. None proved particularly successful—computers in particular entailed large losses—and AT&T remained dependent on the increasingly competitive long-distance telephone market for its profits. Reorganization was a tool, and the results depended on the skill of those who wielded it. Still, in able hands, it allowed U.S. companies to respond vigorously to changing circumstances.

Changes in research and development programs represent another example of increased focus. In the 1970s R&D outlays in the United States had declined to about 2.2 percent of GDP, a drop of roughly 20 percent from the 1960s, largely because of lower federal spending on defense research and the space program. In the 1980s outlays returned to the old level, between 2.6 and 2.7 percent of GDP, but the structure of research was different. Industry itself provided a growing portion of total expenditure, outspending government for the first time in 1980, and by 2000 providing two and a half times as much money as Washington. In contrast to the 1960s and 1970s, most companies shied away from basic research, which might provide gigantic breakthroughs but usually delivered nothing. They left such projects to government and universities, instead choosing research that promised incremental improvements in existing technology. This approach might be less exciting than basic research, but the economic returns were usually greater.

FINANCE

Financial markets played a key role in corporate reorganization. Companies seeking to refine their focus depended on the mergers and acquisitions departments of investment banks to execute their plans. Less important but more dramatic, some financiers initiated reorganizations themselves. Equity prices were stagnant in the 1970s, held down by economic uncertainty. As a result, by the 1980s the stock market capitalization of many firms was below the value of their physical assets. Clever financiers took advantage of this situation, purchasing companies and then selling off their assets for a substantial profit, often borrowing funds to finance the operation—so-called leveraged

buyouts. Some kept choice properties for themselves and gradually accumulated business empires. Conglomerates were particularly attractive targets because such companies were rarely able
to get maximum returns from all their various divisions. A basic
disconnect in securities markets facilitated takeovers. A small in-
vestor unhappy with a company's management could do little
but sell the stock, depressing the price. But a financier with sufficient resources could actually purchase a company and install
new management that, presumably, would deliver higher earnings. Such an individual could afford to pay an above-market
price for the company's depressed stock—delighting investors—
while still making a large profit. The 1980s saw a series of ever-
larger buyouts orchestrated by specialized firms like Kohlberg,
Kravis, Roberts (KKR) and Forstman, Little. The process culminated in the famous 1988 battle for control of RJR/Nabisco,
which sold cigarettes and food. After a round of frenzied bidding, the company fetched more than $20 billion.

These transactions generated tremendous controversy. In
some cases financiers initiated buyouts not to take control of a
company but to force its management to buy their stock at a premium, a practice known as "greenmail." Executives would agree
to this because a successful buyout might well cost them their
jobs. Such a transaction benefited the financiers, who made large
profits, and managers, who remained employed. But it hurt
shareholders, who often saw the value of their stock fall. It could
also permanently weaken a firm. The chemical producer Union
Carbide made a huge one-time payment to stockholders to fend
off an unwanted buyer in the early 1980s. To finance this it sold
off its profitable consumer goods divisions, which among other
things made batteries and garbage bags, sacrificing its most
promising avenue for future growth.

The operations of firms like KKR and Forstman, Little,
which eschewed greenmail, received criticism too. Such firms

ruthlessly cut costs at the companies they acquired, often dismissing employees wholesale. Naturally, many found the picture of
financiers earning millions while depriving people of their jobs
offensive. But however distasteful, properly executed downsizing strengthened companies and the economy as a whole. And
companies like KKR earned their greatest profits when they actually made firms more efficient. But such operations often ran
into problems. Even savvy purchasers often failed to understand
the subtler workings of the corporations they purchased, not dis-
tinguishing between necessary and wasteful expenses. As a result
they sometimes overestimated the savings they could realize,
which led them to pay too much. To cover the purchase price,
buyers then had to cut costs in ways that weakened firms. In extreme cases buyers saddled companies with debts they could not
pay, eventually leading to bankruptcy.

Even omitting greenmail, buyouts presented a mixed picture.
In many cases they performed a service, breaking up unwieldy
conglomerates or forcing bloated firms to reduce costs. But not
every firm involved actually needed reorganization. Many oil
companies became targets simply because falling petroleum
prices had depressed their stock price, not because their management was weak. And buyers often loaded firms with too much
debt, leading to collapse. Some firms eventually recovered from
bankruptcy, but many did not. The pace of leveraged buyouts
slowed sharply after 1990. Rising stock prices made it harder to
find undervalued companies, while several large buyouts ended
in default, discouraging lenders from financing such operations.

Although buyouts generated the most attention, after 1982 financial markets boomed across the board. In the 1970s stock
prices had stagnated, and between 1970 and 1974 the number of
Americans who owned stocks had actually declined—the only
such drop in the post-1945 era. By the early 1980s, however,
falling inflation and economic recovery had made equities once

again attractive. The Fed's decision to cut interest rates in the summer of 1982 touched off a rally that lasted, with some fits and starts, to the end of the decade. The Dow Jones industrial average, a little above 800 in 1982, peaked at 4000 in 1990. A spectacular market crash in October 1987, which at the time seemed disastrous, had little long-term impact. Large gains attracted new investors, and the volume of trading surged to levels unimaginable just a few years earlier. Even during the most frenetic period in the 1960s, trading on the New York Stock Exchange had rarely exceeded 20 million shares a day. By the mid-1980s trading topped 100 million shares a day, and by the end of the century, 1 billion shares were routinely changing hands on the NYSE each day. The NASDAQ market, an electronic trading system created by the National Association of Securities Dealers (NASD) in 1971, also expanded rapidly, briefly approaching the volume of the NYSE in the late 1990s before falling back.

Bond markets enjoyed comparable growth. Government deficits required Washington to issue a great many bonds; the dollar value of federal debt tripled in the 1980s. Perhaps more important over the long run, a large market developed for bonds backed by home mortgage loans. These instruments, pioneered in the late 1970s and early 1980s by bankers at Salomon Brothers, bundled together home mortgages into securities sold to investors such as insurance companies and pension funds. This market profited from the deteriorating position of Savings & Loans, which held large quantities of mortgages made years before at interest rates well below current levels. In the 1980s S&Ls disposed of many of their mortgages, turning them into bonds and selling them, writing off against taxes the losses thereby incurred and investing the proceeds in other sectors that S&L managers hoped would do better. Eventually almost all home loans were financed in this fashion, winding up in the portfolios of long-term investors—a far more stable system than relying on short-term deposits at S&Ls to finance mortgages. Finally, bond markets gained immensely from the growth of "junk" bonds, an instrument popularized by Michael Milken of the brokers Drexel, Burnham. At any given time only a few hundred of the largest American companies qualify as "investment grade" in the eyes of the agencies that rate debt. All other securities are, in the slang of finance, "junk." But many smaller companies are sound and simply lack the history or size demanded by rating agencies. Milken understood this and underwrote loans for dynamic but untested young firms like MCI, McCaw Cellular, and Turner Broadcasting. Later he financed many of the largest buyouts. By the late 1980s the market for junk bonds was mature enough to survive the collapse of Drexel, Burnham after Milken's conviction for securities fraud.

The growth of mortgage and junk bonds formed part of a broader trend that continued into the 1990s known as "securitization." Investment banks increasingly offered bonds backed by business loans, home mortgages, car notes, and installment credit—the kinds of loans traditionally financed by commercial banks. The process was uneven, in part because those offering securities did not always understand the risks involved, and unexpected losses sometimes developed. Nevertheless over time this trend increased opportunities for both lenders and borrowers by widening the market for loans. It also helps account for reductions in the regulatory barriers between investment and commercial banking. As their businesses merged, it seemed pointless to maintain distinctions between these institutions.

THIRD WORLD DEBT AND THE ISSUE OF DEVELOPMENT

In international trade and finance, many of the trends evident during the 1970s reversed themselves during the 1980s.

In the 1970s developing countries profited from high prices for the commodities they exported as well as from easy credit that let them borrow on good terms against future earnings. Conditions were so good that many politicians and analysts in both the third world and the developed countries believed that the balance of economic power had shifted away from the industrial nations to commodity producers. The 1980–1982 recession brutally rebuked this idea. Commodity prices collapsed even as interest rates went to previously unimagined levels, sharply raising the cost of borrowing. Even the once-powerful OPEC found that members were ignoring its directives, selling petroleum below its agreed-upon price. These developments badly hurt commodity-producing regions of the United States, but at least these belonged to a larger nation willing to offer help and able to absorb excess workers. Developing countries had no such resource.

Attention quickly focused on the debt of third world countries. By 1982 Mexico and Brazil each owed $80 billion to creditors in the industrial democracies, Argentina owed $40 billion, and many other developing countries owed lesser but substantial sums. With commodity prices falling and the cost of money rising, countries could no longer pay even the interest on these debts, much less the principal. Realizing this, lenders refused to extend new credits. In 1982 Mexico defaulted on its debts, and most other third world borrowers seemed ready to follow.

The situation alarmed the American government. U.S. banks were among the chief creditors of these countries. Many of these banks had suffered serious losses in the 1980–1982 recession, and third world default might well bankrupt them. Political considerations figured as well. The cold war intensified during the first half of the 1980s, and Washington saw the third world, and particularly Latin America, as a major battleground. Economic chaos there would strengthen the appeal of communism. Mexico, one of the chief debtors, shared a long border with the United

States, and unrest to the south would almost certainly affect the northern neighbor.

Initially authorities sought simply to avoid default. Banks and the industrial democracies, usually working through the IMF, extended debtor countries new credits large enough to cover the interest on outstanding loans. Third world governments cut spending and raised taxes to improve their financial position, and banks with outstanding loans increased reserves against losses so that, if default did occur, they would survive. Such measures staved off immediate disaster, but they did not solve the problems of developing nations. Commodity prices were low and foreign capital was unavailable—new loans did little more than allow for the payment of interest on old borrowing. Developing countries had trouble financing even basic imports, and companies in these nations that relied on foreign supplies found costs escalating sharply. Financial retrenchment designed to remedy this problem cut deeply into domestic consumption, crippling firms that serviced the home market. Output and income fell in many third world countries. Some estimates suggest that in the 1980s per capita income in Mexico fell by half, and other countries fared as poorly.

Meanwhile the "Four Tigers" of Asia—South Korea, Taiwan, Hong Kong, and Singapore—had begun to assert themselves. Possessing few natural resources, they had instead concentrated on building up export industries. Initially they emphasized labor-intensive sectors like textiles, apparel, and shoes because they had large, poor populations in need of work. In time, however, these countries developed more sophisticated industries. By the 1980s they were selling not only textiles and shoes but also automobiles, videocassette recorders, and microprocessors throughout North America and Europe. Most notably, their per capita incomes were approaching those of the developed countries.

Their success, coupled with disastrous conditions in much of the rest of the third world, led to a radical shift in thinking about economic development. After 1945, thought on the matter had emphasized "import substitution." Supposedly governments could best promote development by protecting and subsidizing domestic industries that competed against imports. If necessary, authorities should create state-owned firms to do this. Developing countries should view foreign investment warily because it allowed foreigners to siphon off the profits of domestic industry. Some countries, most notably Mexico and Brazil, had a measure of success with these policies, building substantial bases of industry. But import substitution had limits. Shielded from foreign competition, companies often drifted into inefficiency, and the relatively small size of domestic markets limited their growth. During the 1980s, with the example of the Four Tigers before them, developing countries began to adopt a new economic strategy dubbed "liberalization," which relied on exports and foreign investment to drive growth and development. Mexico, which began reform in earnest after a devastating earthquake wrecked much of Mexico City in 1985, offered perhaps the most dramatic example. Since the 1930s the Mexican government had protected domestic firms from foreign competition, regulated prices and wages, and owned and managed the transportation system, the oil industry, and other businesses. After 1985, however, it began to dismantle these restrictions, in particular encouraging foreign companies to set up assembly plants to take advantage of Mexico's large, inexpensive labor force. The government also sold off its industrial holdings except in petroleum, which was politically sensitive, and in general reduced its regulation of business.

The success of such policies depended on the response of the United States and other industrial countries. By definition, developing nations lack adequate capital and markets. The industrial democracies are the best source of both, and liberalization represented an attempt to tap into these resources. Such efforts impose costs on the industrialized nations. Imports from developing countries displace domestic products, and foreign borrowers compete with domestic ones. But the long-term benefits of third world development are substantial because as these countries produce more, they also consume more, offering new markets. In the short run, however, the losses can be more obvious than the gains.

The United States generally accommodated developing countries. It allowed foreign firms that met U.S. accounting standards to issue bonds and stock in New York. Although imports to the United States did face restrictions—limits on textiles were a particularly contentious point—the country's markets remained comparatively open. A major advance occurred in 1992 when Washington signed a free-trade pact with Mexico, eliminating most barriers to trade in goods and services between the two countries and harmonizing regulations that affected trade in a number of areas.

THE TRIALS OF GEORGE BUSH

Economic policy during George Bush's administration suffered from two weaknesses. Bush owed his elevation to the presidency in 1988 to his close association with the popular Reagan, whom he had served as vice president. He promised to continue his predecessor's policies—indeed, Bush's most famous statement during the 1988 campaign, "Read my lips, no new taxes!" reaffirmed his commitment to Reagan's tax cuts. Yet Bush disagreed with Reagan on some aspects of economic policy—in particular the federal deficit worried him. Perhaps more important, Bush was not that interested in economic issues. He focused on foreign policy, in particular on managing the disintegration of the Soviet Union and on waging the Gulf War against

Iraq. Despite some valuable initiatives, the president never devised and promoted a coherent general economic program.

The Bush administration spent much of its time sorting out problems inherited from Reagan. First, it had to deal with the collapse of the Savings & Loan industry. The sharp rise of interest rates in the 1970s and early 1980s had badly hurt S&Ls, which had to pay depositors high rates but faced stagnant earnings on mortgage loans made years earlier at lower, fixed rates. In the early 1980s Congress attempted to rescue these institutions by allowing them to diversify their portfolios, and in response many S&Ls sold off their home mortgages (at a loss) and put the money into commercial real estate and junk bonds. But S&L executives rarely understood these fields, and many of their investments failed. By 1989 a large portion of these institutions were bankrupt, with liabilities greater than their assets. The federal insurance of deposits allowed S&Ls to continue to operate, but the longer they remained open, the greater their losses. In 1989 President Bush secured from Congress a bill creating a new bureau of the Federal Deposit Insurance Corporation (FDIC), the Resolution Trust Corporation, with authority to close bankrupt S&Ls and pay off their depositors in full, and the measure appropriated sufficient funds to accomplish this. The FDIC spent more than $200 billion closing troubled institutions, though it eventually recouped about half that sum from the sale of S&L assets. Depositors suffered no losses, but stockholders in failed S&Ls received nothing.

The Bush administration also dealt effectively with the festering problem of third world debt. By 1989 the situation had improved somewhat. Institutions like Citibank and the Bank of America, with large loans to countries such as Mexico and Brazil, had made substantial provisions against losses, so they could write off most of their third world debt without fear of bankruptcy or even great damage to their earnings. Many debtors had also strengthened their position. Thanks to a mixture of liberalization and government economies, many Latin American countries had reached a point where they could pay their current expenses, except for interest on loans, without borrowing. Conditions were propitious for a settlement. The Treasury Department, led by Secretary James Brady, took the initiative. It brokered a series of agreements under which creditors agreed to forgive roughly half of what was owed them in exchange for "Brady bonds" covering the rest. Through a series of complex financial maneuvers, the U.S. government guaranteed the principal of these bonds at maturity (usually about twenty years), though not the interest until then.

These accords substantially boosted the economies of Latin America. Liberalization, by eliminating many restrictions on domestic and foreign business, had created new opportunities for investment, and the resolution of outstanding debts encouraged foreign and domestic entrepreneurs to take advantage of these. This investment touched off a boom and substantially upgraded Latin American industry. The economies of this region would experience plenty of difficulties in the 1990s, but it was nevertheless an era of progress—something few would say for the 1980s. Yet conditions in some debtor countries—most notably in sub-Saharan Africa—remained so bad that settlement was impossible, even at the rate of fifty cents on the dollar. These areas did not recover.

The final problem the Bush administration inherited from its predecessor, the budget deficit, proved the most difficult. Political factors were the chief barrier to action. During the second half of the 1980s economic growth, limits on spending increases, and higher revenue from the 1986 tax reform had allowed progress against the deficit, which by 1989 had fallen to about $150 billion, or 3 percent of GDP. But entitlement spending—most notably health care and old-age pensions—continued to increase automatically while tax revenue had ceased to grow as a portion of GDP. Further progress against the deficit would therefore require higher taxes, reductions in entitlements, or both. But Republicans remained staunchly opposed to the former, and Democrats, who had solid majorities in both houses of Congress, refused to countenance the latter. In 1990, after tortuous negotiations, Congress finally enacted a compromise that limited future spending, including Medicare and Medicaid (but not Social Security pensions), and raised the income tax on earnings over $85,000 from 28 percent to 31 percent. Estimates suggested that the measure would cut federal borrowing by a total of $500 billion over the next five years. One-third of savings would come from higher taxes, the rest from spending reductions.

President Bush paid a high political price for this accomplishment. Many conservative Republicans complained that he had betrayed them by accepting tax hikes, and they refused to support the final legislation, or did so only grudgingly. The conservative Patrick Buchanan later challenged Bush for the 1992 Republican nomination. Buchanan's gambit failed, but it greatly complicated the president's reelection effort. Bush did not even get credit for taking a politically difficult step to reduce the deficit. In the 1992 election, the independent Ross Perot, who based his campaign on deficit reduction, won nearly 20 percent of the vote.

The conservative revolt against the Bush administration indicates the degree to which tax reduction had become an article of faith among Republicans. Lower taxes represented the most dramatic domestic accomplishment of the Reagan administration, and Reagan was the standard against which conservative Republicans measured themselves. Just as every Democratic president in the generation after the Great Depression had his own version of Franklin D. Roosevelt's New Deal—Truman's Fair Deal, Kennedy's New Frontier, Johnson's Great Society—so too did every ambitious Republican in the generation following Reagan have a program of tax cuts. But tax cuts were not always appropriate. By reducing the highest marginal rate from 70 to 28 percent, the Reagan administration no doubt significantly stimulated enterprise. By 1990, however, the deficit was a far greater problem than a 31 percent income tax rate.

The Bush administration launched some new initiatives, but the president could not always give them the time and effort required for success, and the Democrats who controlled Congress usually refused to cooperate, for both political and ideological reasons. The effort to cut the capital gains tax represents a good example. Traditionally capital gains—profits from the sale of investments—had enjoyed special status, with the government claiming far less of it than regular income. The 1986 tax reform had ended this situation, however, grouping capital gains with other income. As such, tax rates on capital gains had actually increased in 1986, from 20 percent to 28 percent. Economic growth requires investment, and capital gains taxes represent a levy on investment. Most other industrial nations did not tax long-term capital gains at all. The administration consistently advocated reducing this tax, but the president never laid out his case to the public in a compelling fashion, and nothing less than strong public pressure would have led congressional Democrats to reduce levies on the holders of wealth. The president secured only a symbolic victory. The 1990 deficit-reduction package left the top rate on capital gains at 28 percent even as it raised that on all other forms of income to 31 percent, reestablishing the principle of a separate rate for capital gains. Nevertheless the rate itself remained unchanged.

This example is not unique. In 1992 the administration negotiated an agreement with Mexico to extend to it the free-trade zone that existed between the United States and Canada. But President Bush did not submit the accord to Congress for approval and did little to secure public support for it—these tasks he left to his successor. The 1990 Clean Air Act represented a great accomplishment, tightening rules on pollution even while minimizing the cost of cleanup. Most notably, the measure allowed companies to trade emissions. A firm able to reduce its pollution inexpensively could cut pollution below the legally required level, selling the margin between its actual and required emissions to a company that could not reduce pollution so easily. This approach encouraged environmental cleanup to follow the least expensive path. But the president did not seek to apply this promising approach to other areas of environmental regulation.

The economy slipped into recession in 1990. The downturn was not nearly as bad as those of 1973–1975 or 1980–1982—unemployment peaked in 1992 around 7.5 percent, compared with 9 percent and 11 percent in the earlier downturns. Nevertheless, for a president elected in large part on the promise to maintain prosperity, the results were devastating. The recession probably cost George Bush reelection in 1992.

Several factors accounted for the downturn. The sharp jump in oil prices following the Iraqi invasion of Kuwait in August 1990 precipitated the recession. Problems went deeper, however. Years of economic growth had created shortages in some areas that showed up in higher prices. The Federal Reserve, under its new leader Alan Greenspan, whom Reagan had appointed to replace the retiring Volcker in 1987, raised interest rates in 1988 and 1989 to contain inflation. The short-term cost of money went from over 5 percent to over 8 percent. In other areas, particularly commercial real estate, new investment had glutted markets, forcing sharp reductions in capital spending. Changes in tax laws intensified this problem. The 1981 tax cut had offered investors in real estate benefits so generous that many developers had initiated projects despite the lack of prospective tenants. The 1986 tax-reform legislation had abruptly terminated these concessions.

Without these tax breaks, many office buildings and shopping malls suddenly became unprofitable, bankrupting developers and stifling new projects. In the long run the change was wise— no country should erect buildings that will stand empty—but the transition was painful.

The Bush administration had no response to the downturn. Normally a president would have asked Congress for tax cuts and spending increases to stimulate the economy. But the large federal deficit would have made such action difficult even had Bush not already made deficit reduction a priority, and congressional Democrats had no interest in stimulative measures that might revive the economy in time to secure Bush's reelection. Nor could the president argue that the elements for a recovery were in place and that the country needed to "stay the course"— because he had not clearly articulated a course. The president's chief response to the recession was to scold the Fed for not cutting interest rates more aggressively. Rates did come down, but not fast enough to rescue Bush. Recovery began in 1992, but at first it was sluggish, with unemployment remaining high well into 1993. Democrat Bill Clinton won election as president in 1992 on the unofficial slogan, "It's the economy, stupid."

5

The "New Economy"

BETWEEN 1992 and 2000 the United States enjoyed extraordinary prosperity, on a par with that of the 1960s. Almost every index of economic well-being advanced. Even worker productivity began to improve after two decades of sluggish growth. Advances in information technology played a critical role in the boom, and many enthusiasts claimed that computers had inaugurated a "New Economy" immune to recession. More thoughtful observers hoped that the boom represented a return to the sort of stable prosperity that Americans had enjoyed between 1945 and 1973, when steadily rising productivity had allowed ever-higher living standards.

REFORM AND DEFICITS

In the first half of the 1990s public investment again dominated economic debate. As the Democratic presidential candidate in 1992, Bill Clinton proposed "investing in the common, national economic resources that enable every person and every firm to create wealth and value. Our productivity and income have been growing so slowly because we've stopped investing in the economic infrastructure that binds our markets and businesses together." In particular Clinton and some of his advisers, like Robert Reich and Laura Tyson, placed special weight on how public investment in education and transportation would improve the productivity of the private sector.

In the context of the early 1990s, public investment had great appeal. It fit easily into American traditions—government had long financed public education and public works such as the interstate highway system. And public investment would address at least one undeniable problem: American primary and secondary schools were not particularly good. In tests of knowledge, U.S. students consistently scored below students in most other industrial countries. Nor did the United States coordinate technical training well with the needs of industry. Significant improvement in these fields would almost certainly strengthen the economy—a better-educated and trained worker is more productive. Perhaps most important, public investment offered to reconcile economic change with social stability. In the 1980s political dialogue had seemed to offer Americans two options: permit change, with all the pain of downsizing and reorganization, or block it and forgo the advantages of new techniques and technology. Public investment promised a third option, easing the hardship of change without obstructing it. For instance, government could train workers laid off from steel mills or auto plants for jobs in the rapidly growing computer industry.

Strong objections did exist. With government running a huge deficit, where would the money for investment come from? The United States spent as much or more on education per pupil as other industrial countries. Republicans contended that weakness in this field reflected not insufficient funding but poor organization. The chief responsibility for education and public works had traditionally resided with the states, not the federal government. Was it appropriate or even practical for Washington to take the lead in these areas? In fact, advocates of public investment offered few specific examples of projects they would undertake, confining themselves to generalities.

Upon taking office in early 1993, President Clinton went in an entirely different direction, focusing on the federal deficit and private investment. "If you bring the deficit down," the president claimed, "You free up money [for] private investment at lower interest rates." This reflected the influence of Robert Rubin, an investment banker who would become Treasury secretary, and Fed chairman Alan Greenspan. In his first year in office the president steered through Congress a deficit-reduction package to cut federal borrowing by $500 billion over the next five years. Although the measure did limit spending, higher taxes provided two-thirds of deficit reduction. The package raised levies on gasoline and increased the tax on incomes above $180,000 from 31 to 36 percent and on incomes above $250,000 from 31 to almost 40 percent.

The administration considered its program a great success. The deficit fell steadily, and in fiscal 1999 the federal government ran a surplus for the first time since 1969. This reflected both higher taxes and lower spending. In 2000 federal taxes took more than 20 percent of GDP, the highest level ever, while Washington's outlays fell to 18.1 percent of GDP for the first time since the mid-1960s. With the federal government borrowing less, interest rates fell to the lowest level in a generation. Private investors took advantage of low rates to borrow and invest, and the economy boomed.

Critics of the Clinton administration argued that the boom created the federal surplus, not the other way around. Federal borrowing began to fall substantially only after 1995, coinciding with a sharp improvement in the growth of productivity and income. They argued that this growth, not higher taxes, provided revenue to balance the budget. Another factor beyond the control of the Clinton administration, the end of the cold war, also boosted government finances. With the Soviet threat gone, defense spending fell to the lowest level, in terms of percent of GDP, since the 1930s.

The truth was more complex than either the Clinton administration or its critics would admit. During the 1990s the United States enjoyed a virtuous cycle. New technologies and techniques provided great opportunities for investment; higher capital spending spurred growth; growth increased federal revenue; higher revenue reduced the deficit; and cheaper money facilitated new investment. This would have happened without the 1990 and 1993 deficit-reduction packages, but these measures substantially reinforced the cycle, making it stronger than it otherwise would have been.

Clinton's program left no room for public investment. Between 1990 and 1998 federal money available for investment—funds left over after paying for defense, interest on the debt, old-age pensions, and health care—fell as a portion of GDP. Defense outlays fell sharply and tax revenue increased, but because the population was aging, spending on the elderly and on health care consumed any free money. In particular, federal health-care outlays increased from 2.7 percent of GDP in 1990 to 3.8 percent in 1998, or 40 percent. Social Security and Medicare are worthy programs, but few would describe them as investments in the long-term future. President Clinton touted a few high-profile initiatives, such as funding for more teachers and police officers, as fulfilling his promises of public investment, but his administration did not increase the share of national resources going to such programs.

Clinton did propose a thorough overhaul of the health-care system that promised to alter the balance between government and private enterprise. About 15 percent of the American population lacked health insurance, and these people had difficulty getting care. Despite this the United States spent huge sums on

medical care, roughly 12 percent of GDP in 1993. Most other industrial democracies had universal, government-funded health
insurance schemes that absorbed less than 10 percent of GDP—
in some cases much less. The price of medical care in the United
States was rising fast, about 10 percent a year. Growing medical
costs strained the federal budget and imposed a heavy burden on
American firms, which usually provided employees' health insurance. The difficulty stemmed from a basic disconnect in the
industry's structure. Patients and their doctors decided on care,
for which insurance companies or government agencies usually
paid. Consumers had little incentive to worry about costs, while
those who paid the bills had little control over care. Clinton proposed a universal, quasi-public insurance scheme that would
cover everyone and control treatment and costs. The savings
from controls would finance insurance for those without.

The huge size of the American medical system, as well as the
emotional nature of health-care issues, rendered any comprehensive evaluation of the system difficult. Obviously it did not work
particularly well for the 15 percent without insurance. More
broadly, Americans did not, on average, live longer than the people of other industrial nations or even of some rapidly developing
areas like Hong Kong. In a few important measures, like infant
mortality, the United States actually fared worse than most other
industrial countries. But the American health-care system may
have delivered a better quality of life, at least to the 85 percent
with insurance. Hip replacements offer a good example. No one
dies from a bad hip, and replacing one is expensive. Accordingly,
most state-sponsored health insurance schemes, such as those in
Canada and Britain, limited the number of such operations.
Waiting lists stretched for months or even years. But someone
whose hip fails faces crippling pain, and the ready availability of
replacements in the United States benefited these people immensely. The American system may also have speeded the pace

of medical advances. U.S. insurance, government and private, paid suppliers of medical care generously, allowing high profits. With guaranteed profits, companies invested heavily to develop new treatments that promised to generate further earnings. The United States produced a great quantity of innovative drugs and treatments. Of course, patients in other countries benefited from these advances too, but without the profits earned in the American market, improvements might not have occurred. Certainly they would not have occurred as rapidly.

Whatever its practical virtues, the administration's health-care plan was a political disaster. Its provisions were incredibly complex—so much so that even its authors had trouble explaining exactly how it would work. People were naturally reluctant to trust something as important as health care to a system they did not understand. The problem went deeper, however. Although conceding that the system as a whole needed overhaul, most Americans were reasonably happy with their health insurance as it was. The president's plan would restrict their benefits to cover the uninsured minority. Lawmakers defeated Clinton's proposal, and in the November 1994 elections the Republicans won majorities in both houses of Congress for the first time in forty years.

Over the next six years government and private insurers imposed piecemeal reforms that contained rising health-care costs and made insurance somewhat more accessible. For Medicare and Medicaid, Washington tightened a system that paid doctors and hospitals a fixed sum depending on the malady treated and the procedure used. Private insurers increasingly utilized Health Maintenance Organizations (HMOs), which offered care through carefully regulated networks of physicians and hospitals. Such restrictions were unpopular, but they kept the growth of health-care expenses to less than 5 percent a year (before inflation) between 1994 and 1999, a sustainable pace. The

Clinton administration also secured legislation providing insurance for children from low-income families and making it easier for people to keep their health insurance if they changed or lost their jobs. The portion of the population without insurance, however, remained stable.

After 1994 the political system settled into deadlock. In 1995 the new Republican majority in Congress moved aggressively to implement its own ideas about economic policy, enacting a budget that cut spending sharply and reduced taxes. President Clinton vetoed the package. These events set the pattern for the rest of the Clinton administration: the president blocked GOP plans for tax cuts, and Congress ignored the administration's spending proposals. Although uncomfortable for the participants, this equilibrium contributed to the reduction of the federal deficit. Certainly the public appeared satisfied—Clinton and most Republicans in Congress easily won reelection in 1996.

Republicans did manage, with the president's acquiescence, to enact some significant economic reforms. They reduced the capital gains tax on investments held for more than a year to 20 percent. Deregulation continued, most notably in banking and telecommunications—legislation weakened or eliminated barriers between different types of businesses in these sectors. For instance, investment and commercial banks gained the right to offer many of the same services, and television networks could purchase more broadcast stations.

Perhaps most important, Congress overhauled farm policy, scrapping much of the structure established in the 1930s during the New Deal. Ideology played a large part in this decision—many Republicans disliked the idea of the government setting prices and output for a large sector of the economy. But practical concerns played a role too. As constituted, federal agricultural programs discouraged farmers from switching to more profitable crops because the government tied benefits to whatever they had traditionally grown. New international conditions posed the most immediate and important challenge, however. Traditionally federal policy had sought both to keep prices high and to encourage exports—two objectives often in conflict. Washington had attempted to resolve the contradiction by subsidizing exports in various ways, but trade agreements increasingly restricted these devices. The American government acquiesced to such restrictions because most other industrial countries protected and subsidized their farmers even more heavily than did the United States, and the elimination of such practices would open large markets abroad for U.S. growers, who were among the world's most efficient producers of many crops. To take advantage of these opportunities, however, domestic farm policy had to change. Congress largely dismantled federal controls on planting, marketing, and pricing, instead offering farmers unconditional payments over several years to ease the transition to a free market. But the hoped-for end to subsidies failed to materialize; Congress actually increased farm subsidies rather than letting them lapse.

The executive branch managed anti-trust and labor policy with little interference from Congress, but in practice the Clinton administration changed little. The administration did not obstruct the wave of mergers that had begun in the 1980s and that, if anything, intensified in the 1990s. A suit against Microsoft represented the major exception to this tolerant anti-trust policy. The government argued that the software giant was using its monopoly of operating systems for personal computers (Windows) to dominate other segments of the market, most notably Internet browsers. For its part, Microsoft contended that a common operating system represented a huge boon to the computer industry and that browsers were an integral part of any such system. After a series of long, expensive, and often obscure legal battles, the government forced Microsoft to change some of its policies, but it was not clear that these significantly altered the company's position.

The Clinton administration put greater effort into labor policy. Its appointees to the National Labor Relations Board interpreted the law more favorably toward unions than had Reagan and Bush officials, and organized labor won some widely publicized disputes, most notably one with Bridgestone Tire. The country's chief labor organization, the American Federation of Labor/Congress of Industrial Organizations (AFL-CIO), elected a more militant leadership that promised to revive the movement. Nevertheless union membership as a percentage of the workforce continued to decline, falling from 16 percent in 1990 to 14 percent by 2000 despite prosperity and declining unemployment after 1992, conditions that usually favored organized labor. The economic factors that had worked against unions in the 1980s—stiff competition, foreign and domestic, and the growth of service industries—still operated in the 1990s, and there was no political support for the sort of radical measures—such as limits on companies' right to lay off workers—that might have reversed the situation.

Political deadlock and the emphasis on deficit reduction further elevated the status of the Federal Reserve. With deficit-reduction packages making spending and taxes inflexible, the central bank had to manage short-term economic policy on its own, adjusting interest rates and monetary growth to keep output expanding and prices stable. Indeed, the Clinton administration's entire economic program hinged on the Fed reducing interest rates as the deficit fell. The central bank managed its responsibilities well, allowing interest rates to decline substantially over the course of the decade, fueling growth. Fed chairman Alan Greenspan recognized earlier than most of his contemporaries that structural changes allowed the economy to grow more rapidly in the 1990s than it had in the 1970s and 1980s, and the central bank adjusted monetary policy accordingly.

THE NEW ECONOMY

Growth in the United States between 1992 and 2000 averaged more than 4 percent a year while unemployment gradually declined to 4 percent, the lowest level since the late 1960s. The rate of inflation actually slowed during the boom. Perhaps most important, productivity began to grow more rapidly, expanding at a 2.6 percent annual rate between 1995 and 2000 and allowing a substantial expansion of real (inflation-adjusted) income. The expansion depended chiefly on monetary policy, the stimulus provided by cheap money, because the 1990 and 1993 deficit-reduction packages, by raising taxes and trimming spending, had retarded the overall demand for goods and services. Fortunately opportunities for profitable capital spending abounded, and business took advantage of low interest rates to borrow and invest. Between 1992 and 2000 capital spending increased from 13.4 percent of GDP to almost 18 percent, with outlays growing every year between 1992 and 2000.

Information technology drove the expansion, playing the same role in the 1990s that railroads had a century earlier. It was the core of what some dubbed the "New Economy." Between 1992 and 2000 total revenue in information technology, including broadcasting and telephones, grew from $371 billion to $815 billion. In 1997 American factories shipped $78.5 billion in semiconductors and $66 billion in computers, up 144 and 66 percent, respectively, from 1992. Much of this growth represented the development of new industries. In the 1990s satellite television first became available in convenient packages at reasonable prices, offering serious competition to cable. The number of cellular phones in use grew from 5.2 million in 1990 to 109.5 million in 2000, a twentyfold increase.

Perhaps more important, however, information technology changed established industries. The effect of checkout scanners on retailing provides a good example. By using a laser to read bar codes on items purchased by consumers, these devices automatically totaled the bill. This not only sped checkout but also allowed retailers to track inventory instantly, reducing the need to count stock—a slow, labor-intensive process. Better information on inventory and sales also permitted retailers to gauge their own purchases more carefully, aligning orders more closely with consumer demand. This allowed a more rapid turnover of inventory, making entire stores and warehouses more efficient. Such technology first became available in the 1970s, but it took retailers years to fully master it. Wal-Mart's early success with scanners is one of the reasons why, by the 1990s, it was the world's largest retailer.

Dell Computer's assembly-to-order system represented perhaps the most dramatic instance of computers transforming production. Dell put together personal computers only as it received orders, producing a wide variety of machines tailored to consumers' specific requests. It did this on an assembly line, using computers to inform everyone along the line what machines needed what components. This system allowed Dell to satisfy the exact demands of consumers and to eliminate product inventory, with all its expenses, even while maintaining the efficiencies of mass production. Dell, which did not exist in 1980, twenty years later had sales of $25 billion.

These developments reflected a new approach to productivity. Mass production, which had dominated thinking on the subject through much of the twentieth century, had broken the process of making goods and services down into its component parts, allowing workers and machines to specialize. Greater specialization made both more efficient. By the 1970s, however, this approach seems to have reached the point of diminishing returns. In the 1990s companies sought to use resources—whether warehouses, machine tools, or people—ever more intensively by carefully managing information. Ford's just-in-time inventories, Dell's assembly-to-order production, and Wal-Mart's inventory-control system were all examples of this approach. Computers were vital to the process because only they could manage information on the scale and with the speed required.

Application of information technology may explain the most encouraging economic advance of the 1990s: more rapid productivity growth. Between 1995 and 2000 output per worker grew at a 2.6 percent annual rate, fast enough to double income in less than thirty years. By contrast the rate of productivity growth between 1973 and 1994, which averaged between 1 and 1.5 percent annually, would have required between fifty and seventy-five years to double real income. Manufacturing productivity grew even faster than in the 1980s while services, where output per worker had been stagnant for years, also registered solid improvement. Some economists argued that higher productivity in the late 1990s was simply a fluke reflecting low oil prices and cheap money. Others pointed to demographics, noting that whereas the workforce had grown 23 percent between 1975 and 1985, it expanded only 14 percent between 1985 and 1995. With fewer new workers, companies had a stronger incentive to improve the output of those on hand. No doubt these factors had an impact. But another school of economic thought argued that better productivity reflected chiefly the more effective application of information technology. According to proponents of this view, who included Alan Greenspan, information technology had the power to transform almost every aspect of economic life, much as the steam engine and electric power once had. Like the steam engine and electricity, however, the full understanding of this technology required decades. Computers first became available in the 1950s, the argument went, but only in the 1990s did business begin fully to exploit their possibilities.

Not only the application but also the power of information technology expanded dramatically in the 1990s. Microcomputers and their software improved immensely, and fiber-optic cable greatly increased the reliability, speed, and volume of communications. The Internet offered alluring possibilities even while demonstrating the difficulties of exploiting new technology. The Defense Department created the forerunner of the Internet in the late 1960s to allow rapid communication between its contractors. The government gradually relinquished control of nonmilitary aspects of the system between 1983 and 1994, allowing commercial interests to exploit the new medium. In 1993 the Mosaic program, the forerunner of Netscape Navigator, became available, allowing those with a computer and a modem to "surf" the Internet. Soon millions of people were sending e-mail and gleaning information from Internet "web sites." By the late 1990s the Internet had become the focus of an extraordinary speculative boom. Convinced of the new medium's unlimited potential, investors poured money into new companies organized to exploit it, particularly as a retailing tool. The frenzy exceeded even the speculative excesses of the late 1960s. New companies that had never earned a profit found their stock worth billions of dollars in financial markets. Telecommunications companies, counting on growing Internet traffic, laid thousands of miles of fiber-optic cable. Inevitably the boom ended badly. Few Internet companies actually made money, and in 2000 they began to go bankrupt by the hundreds. Communications firms discovered that they had vastly overestimated demand, leaving themselves with far more fiber-optic cable than they needed. On paper, total losses ran into the tens of billions of dollars—and no doubt contributed greatly to the recession that began in 2001. But however exaggerated, the

Internet boom was not a total waste. Some viable companies like America On Line (AOL), Ebay, Amazon.com, and Yahoo! did emerge. Despite the financial collapse, Internet use continued to grow. The Internet was clearly a useful tool, allowing cheap, instant communication and the rapid transmission and update of information. But mastery of the technology would take time.

Heavy investment in information technology drove a broad-based economic expansion. Automobile sales grew to around sixteen million units a year. The greatest profits were in the sport utility vehicle (SUV) category, which American firms dominated. Sales of such vehicles more than doubled between 1990 and 2000. Low interest rates encouraged the construction and renovation of houses. Emblematic of this, Home Depot, which sold building supplies in warehouse-sized stores, became one of the country's largest retailers in the 1990s. Even genetic engineering began to demonstrate some of the promise of which boosters had been speaking for years, with firms such as Monsanto offering farmers genetically engineered seeds that resisted pests and herbicides.

Unlike the 1980s, no glaring exceptions marred the image of prosperity. By the mid-1990s downsizing was largely complete. Economic change continued, and companies hired and fired accordingly. But in contrast to the 1980s, business had no great backlog of adjustments to make. Many traditional manufacturing firms that had struggled in the 1980s did well in the 1990s, thanks in part to successful efforts to reduce costs and upgrade products and production. Again unlike the 1980s, the income of the poorest 20 percent of the population grew in the 1990s. The benefits of prosperity still went disproportionately to the wealthy—the distribution of income remained stable after 1993—but the share going to the bottom 20 percent of families ceased shrinking, and higher productivity allowed better wages across the board.

After shifting in favor of those at the top for more than fifteen years, why did the distribution of income suddenly stabilize after 1993? Many observers credited tax increases on the wealthy enacted in 1990 and 1993, but because figures on income distribution do not take taxes into account, this is unlikely. Probably more important, the Bush and Clinton administrations both increased the minimum wage, which had remained unchanged during the 1980s. This translated into substantial raises for many who held low-paying jobs. Moreover the growing scale of information technology industries allowed a broader segment of the population to enjoy the benefits of their expansion, and the relative stability of manufacturing meant that the number of well-paying jobs for semi-skilled workers stopped declining and may even have increased somewhat. Finally, the number of single-parent households apparently stopped growing.

Financial markets reflected good times. In 1999 the Dow Jones industrial average pierced 11,000, almost three times its 1990 high, while the NASDAQ, which listed many information technology stocks, surged from 1,000 to 5,000 over the same period. The pace of mergers and acquisitions was, if anything, more rapid than in the 1980s. "Securitization" of consumer and commercial loans became more common. The 1990s did not see financial innovations as important as mortgage or junk bonds, but established lines of business were busy enough to keep investment banks profitable and growing.

Recession punctuated the boom in 2001. At the height of the expansion, some had argued that advances in information technology had rendered the business cycle obsolete. For instance, better control of inventories would supposedly prevent retailers from building up the sort of excess stocks that could force them to cut purchases suddenly, traditionally a forerunner of recession. But as the Internet boom illustrated, high technology and economic irrationality were not mutually exclusive. By 2000 it was clear that the country had far more capacity in many areas of information technology than it needed, discouraging further investment and in some cases driving firms into bankruptcy. At the same time growth had driven up the price of oil and in some areas created shortages of electricity, reducing consumers' discretionary income. In March 2001 the economy began to shrink.

Hard times provide a good gauge of a country's economic strength. Prosperity conceals weaknesses; recession highlights them. By this standard the United States was strong. Unemployment remained below 6 percent in 2001, and despite a few spectacular bankruptcies, the financial system remained stable. Although the devastating terrorist attacks on the World Trade Center and the Pentagon in September 2001 shook financial markets and consumers, both recovered their equilibrium fairly quickly. Perhaps most significantly, productivity continued to expand at a 2.6 percent rate. This represented perhaps the best evidence that higher productivity growth was in fact a long-term development.

GLOBALIZATION

In the 1990s international trade and investment played a larger role in the American economy than at any other time in the twentieth century. Their importance had been growing since at least the 1970s, but in the 1990s the activity took on a new immediacy. Problems such as the energy crisis, inflation, and the budget deficit faded, clearing the way for the emergence of new issues, and emotional debates in 1993 and 1994 over trade agreements focused attention on what observers quickly dubbed "globalization."

American trade grew rapidly. By the end of the century, exports of goods and services totaled more than 10 percent of GDP, and imports were even higher. As recently as 1969, both had been less than 4 percent of GDP. Manufactured products represented by far the largest portion of sales abroad, accounting for 90 percent of goods exported. Considering that manufacturing represented only about a fifth of GDP, these figures suggest that roughly a third of the output of U.S. factories was going to foreign markets. Services performed well too. Americans sold increasing quantities of software, movies, and television programs abroad, as well as business services like banking, advertising, consulting, accounting, and data processing. U.S. shipping firms and airlines also enjoyed substantial foreign earnings, and tourists from other countries flocked to destinations such as Walt Disney World and Las Vegas. The United States enjoyed a large surplus on services, at times as much as 1 percent of GDP, though this was not enough to compensate for the huge deficit on goods.

Trade figures, impressive as they are, do not convey the full impact of globalization. Foreign companies stepped up the construction of plants and offices in the United States, following a trend apparent since at least the 1980s. In 1997 Mercedes opened its first factory outside Germany, in Tuscaloosa, Alabama, a town that the firm's executives had probably not heard of before 1990. Foreign companies also purchased American firms—British Petroleum bought Amoco and Atlantic Richfield—while American firms continued to expand abroad. Globalization also extended to financial markets. The New York Stock Exchange increasingly listed prominent foreign companies like Daimler-Benz and the Deutsche Bank, and foreign investors channeled more money through U.S. equity markets. The NYSE and NASDAQ were the world's largest, most efficient stock markets, and both investors and companies saw advantages to operating through them.

The U.S. payments deficit remained high. It declined during the 1990–1991 recession because American purchases of imported as well as domestic products fell, but by the middle of the decade the United States was again spending more than $100 billion a year abroad in excess of what it earned, a figure that increased through the end of the century. Heavy imports of goods, including raw materials like oil, accounted for the entire shortfall. But these deficits caused far less alarm than those of the 1980s. In part, a decade of deficits had inured Americans to the phenomenon. The U.S. economy was also growing fast, so that in most industries both importers and domestic producers had plenty of business. Sectors like textiles and steel suffered, but overall unemployment remained low, so that displaced workers could usually find new positions—in some cases better-paid ones. For instance, many new foreign plants went into the textile district of the Carolinas. Moreover, economists attributed the size of the American deficit in part to the rapid economic growth of the United States, which in the 1990s outpaced every other major industrial country—even Japan, which in the 1980s had seemed poised to challenge American economic dominance. Rapid expansion and strong demand naturally attracted imports. In fact, sales in the United States were a major source of economic growth for other countries. In this context, deficits could be considered a sign of strength, reflecting superior overall performance. Certainly the United States had no trouble attracting money to finance its deficit—because the American economy was growing so fast and seemed to offer so many opportunities, people were eager to invest in the country. The demand for dollars was so strong that the currency's value actually rose during the second half of the decade even though interest rates fell and the payments deficit expanded.

The Clinton administration encouraged these trends. Like every other administration since World War II, it accepted economic arguments in favor of open trade and calculated that, in the long run, liberalization would benefit the United States by opening foreign markets to American products. In 1993 the administration secured congressional approval for the trade pact with Mexico (the North American Free Trade Agreement, or NAFTA) despite stiff opposition, much of it from Democrats closely allied with labor unions. In 1994 it persuaded Congress to approve an accord creating the World Trade Organization (WTO). The WTO built on the strengths and repaired the weaknesses of the General Agreement on Tariffs and Trade (GATT), which had regulated world trade since the 1940s. The WTO accord not only covered tariffs and quotas but also a host of domestic measures which substantially affected trade, and it created a body to adjudicate disputes between signatories, something GATT had lacked. In many respects it represented an updated version of the International Trade Organization (ITO) of the 1940s, which had failed largely because developing countries refused to forgo protection or to guarantee foreign investment. New thinking on economic development, which emphasized the benefits of trade and foreign investment, was key to the success of the WTO.

The approval of these pacts involved unusually emotional debates in Congress. Since 1945 trade policy had been the province of a few high-ranking officials, assisted or obstructed by the special interests involved. Even the intensification of foreign competition in the 1980s and the discussion of "competitiveness" had spawned no focused debate among the public. But congressional votes, first on the Mexican pact and then on the WTO, quickly became a center of popular political discussion, and the administration secured victory only after an intense effort to sway public opinion. Trade became a political issue in a way it had not been for decades.

The Clinton administration also worked hard to keep the international financial system stable. It contributed funds to rescue Mexico from financial crisis in 1994 and some of the countries of Southeast Asia from an even more severe crisis in 1997. In both cases the nations in question had experienced rapid growth fueled by foreign investment, but their borrowing had reached a point at which lenders began to doubt they could repay the money. Credit had evaporated, creating an economic crisis. To avoid default and a worse panic, the industrial democracies had, through the IMF, extended substantial credits to troubled countries. The Clinton administration also tolerated a surge of imports from these nations after their crises. These countries desperately needed foreign sales to employ their people and foreign exchange to repair their finances. The administration understood this and did not complain about higher imports, even though some U.S. firms suffered.

A few economists criticized such rescue operations for creating "moral hazard." Supposedly, knowledge that the industrial democracies would, through the IMF, rescue a country in trouble made lenders more willing to grant risky loans to developing countries. Bailouts allowed lenders to avoid the consequences of their reckless actions. Without such an implicit guarantee, lenders would presumably allocate credit more carefully, cutting borrowers off before they became overextended and eliminating the need for rescue operations. The industrial democracies need only allow troubled countries to go bankrupt; in the future lenders would become more cautious. The argument had merit, but the American government and the IMF could hardly stand aside while whole economies went bankrupt. This was particularly true if, as in the case of Mexico in 1994 and South Korea in 1997, governments stood ready to make painful adjustments to resolve financial difficulties.

Globalization did encounter opposition. Labor unions and the textile industry constituted a central element of resistance. The textile industry is labor intensive—that is, it uses unskilled labor, and wages are a very large part of its expenses. With a few exceptions, U.S. firms could not compete against textile producers based in third world countries, where wages were quite low. Similar considerations motivated unions. Some of the industries in which organized labor was strong, like steel, had allowed themselves to fall behind foreign producers and had trouble competing effectively. Many companies in these industries would not survive without protection. Even in industries better placed to compete against foreign rivals, like autos, competition from abroad limited what unions could demand from employers.

Another group, perhaps best represented by consumer advocate Ralph Nader, opposed globalization because of a general suspicion of capitalism and, in particular, big business. They did not trust private enterprise and looked to government to limit its abuses. But companies operating across borders could avoid such control. Nader argued that American, European, and Japanese companies invested in developing countries chiefly to exploit cheap labor and less stringent environmental regulations. Thus to permit the import of products from these countries without restriction would either destroy native industry in the developed countries or force labor and environmental standards there down to the level of the poorest, most polluted nations.

Globalization created strange political alliances. The billionaire Ross Perot supported Ralph Nader in his opposition to globalization, warning that free trade with Mexico would create a "giant sucking sound" as plants and jobs moved south. Representative Newt Gingrich, one of President Clinton's harshest critics and the leader of House Republicans, provided critical support for both NAFTA and the WTO pact.

The economics of globalization were clear. Imports displaced domestic products only if they were cheaper or of higher quality and so benefited consumers. In some cases consumers used imports like steel to make their own products, such as machine tools and autos. Forcing them to rely on high-priced domestic suppliers would make it harder for them to compete with foreign rivals. To raise income a society must improve productivity. One way to do this is to move people from labor-intensive industries like textiles to other areas that use workers more efficiently. Globalization advanced this process in the United States, forcing labor-intensive producers out of business and expanding the markets of high-wage industries. For their part, most developing countries had large populations of under- and unemployed people who would appreciate steady work in textile mills and apparel factories. Some countries—notably Italy, Japan, and South Korea—had used such labor-intensive industry as a starting point from which to build sophisticated economies. A wholesale exodus of industry to developing countries, which Ross Perot and many other opponents of globalization anticipated, was unlikely. Critics of globalization confused labor costs with wage levels. Well-paid, highly productive workers in the developed countries could be cheaper than inexpensive, inexperienced workers in the developing ones. And for most companies access to markets, suppliers, raw materials, skilled workers, communications, and transportation were more important than labor costs. Industries like textiles, with its intense focus on wage levels, were the exception. In fact, most foreign investment occurred between industrialized countries, not from them to developing ones.

But the issue was not quite as simple as economics suggests. American workers displaced by imports were often among the least educated and worst paid. They might lack the skills to fill better-paying jobs, even if such were available. Although displaced union members could probably find work, they were unlikely to find new jobs that paid as well as their existing ones. In the third world, industrial development often entailed environmental degradation and exploitation of workers. Factories might lack basic safety features, employ children, and discharge industrial waste without reference to how it affected the environment.

Governments could contain such problems, but in many cases authorities in the third world were incompetent or corrupt. Despite liberalization, the industrialized countries often continued to subsidize their farmers and to restrict imports, particularly of textiles, limiting the gains that developing countries could realize from freer trade.

On international economic policy the Clinton administration took a clear stand. It consistently asserted that, on balance, the growth of international trade and investment benefited the United States. Policy should encourage the most dynamic sectors of the economy, not protect the weakest ones. Clinton's defense of the Mexican treaty and the WTO in the face of strong opposition, much of it from Democrats, represented a triumph of economic principle over political expediency.

In many ways the opposition to globalization was strong. Unions had immense influence among Democrats, and the textile industry had defenders in both parties. Pressure from these interests led Congress to limit President Clinton's ability to negotiate new trade pacts after 1994. Protesters also disrupted some international summits, notably a WTO meeting in Seattle in 1999.

Nevertheless foes of globalization suffered glaring weaknesses. They were a minority. When the American public confronted the issue squarely, as when Congress debated the Mexican treaty in 1993 and the WTO in 1994, opinion supported freer trade. And the passage of time made the reversal of globalization ever less likely as Americans became more reliant both on foreign suppliers for goods and on markets abroad to absorb their own products. The denser this network of relationships, the harder it would be to extract the country from it without massive disruption. Finally, opponents of globalization had only a negative program. Whatever its imperfections, globalization offered both to coordinate the economic interest of the world's nations and to provide an avenue through which third world countries could develop industry. Its critics had no plan for either.

ISSUES AND CAMPAIGNS

In economic terms the 2000 presidential election was anomalous. Prosperity encouraged the candidates to focus on long-term challenges facing the country rather than to seek votes by discussing immediate problems. As a result, the candidates seriously examined what the United States should do over the next fifteen years, at least in some fields.

Demographics offered the greatest concern for the future. Since the 1970s Social Security and Medicare expenses had escalated rapidly as the population aged, growing faster than the economy. Only sharp increases in Social Security taxes, which funded these programs, had kept them solvent. The situation could only grow worse. Nearly one-third of the population had been born between 1945 and 1965, and when these people retired, costs would grow immensely. The rate of economic growth would affect the country's ability to bear these expenses, but no reasonable pace of expansion could increase revenue from Social Security taxes fast enough to save these programs from eventual bankruptcy. What was to be done?

If demography offered the greatest reason for concern, more rapid economic growth—and the budget surplus it created—offered the greatest opportunity. In the late 1990s projections suggested that over the next ten to fifteen years the federal government would run surpluses totaling several trillion dollars. Of course, historically such long-term estimates were unreliable. Even minor changes in economic performance could substantially affect tax revenue, and Congress decided many outlays annually and could easily alter spending, invalidating predictions. Moreover, projections made during the boom of the late 1990s exaggerated likely growth and revenue. Nevertheless higher productivity growth did promise faster expansion of federal revenue after 2000 than during the 1970s and 1980s. Besides, politicians had to base their plans on something, and optimistic projections are more attractive than pessimistic ones.

Democrats wanted to use federal surpluses to repair Social Security. The details and titles of their proposals varied—Vice President Al Gore, the party's presidential candidate in 2000, coined the slogan "lock box" to describe his version. The essence was simple: the government would use its surpluses to pay off the entire federal debt, about $5 trillion, before the baby boomers retired. Then Washington could borrow again on a large scale to pay the pensions and medical expenses of this group as it aged.

The Republicans, led in 2000 by Texas governor George W. Bush, the son of the former president, had a very different plan. They would devote the surplus to tax cuts. Why, they reasoned, should the government take from its citizens money it did not need to fund ongoing operations? The more cynical among them argued that Congress would inevitably spend a surplus rather than save it. The more sophisticated contended that, as in the late 1950s, a long-term imbalance between revenue and spending in favor of the former might well constitute "fiscal drag," retarding demand and slowing economic growth unnecessarily. To rescue Social Security, Bush proposed allowing people to invest a portion of the taxes government collected to fund the system in the stock market, which had historically yielded high returns, rather than in the low-yielding government bonds in which surplus funds were traditionally invested. Higher returns would make the system solvent.

Although Republicans' enthusiasm for tax cuts was hardly new, the Democrats' embrace of budget surpluses was. Since the 1930s Democrats had, with some important exceptions like President Truman, exhibited less concern for fiscal convention than

Republicans. But the Reagan and Clinton administrations had changed things. In the 1980s Democrats realized that financial weakness prevented the federal government from undertaking the sort of new social programs that most Democrats favored—indeed, some believed that the Reagan administration had tolerated deficits in part to preclude such initiatives. In the 1990s Democrats were eager to claim credit for prosperity, and only in fiscal policy had the Clinton administration broken decisively with its Republican predecessors. If Democrats deserved special credit for good times, deficit reduction had to be the cause.

But balanced budgets were no more appropriate to every situation than tax cuts. The large deficits accumulated by Washington in the 1980s and early 1990s were dangerous, at least in the long run, and the Bush and Clinton administrations deserve credit for taking politically difficult steps to contain them. Governments, however, run surpluses during eras of peace and prosperity in part so that they can borrow easily during recession and war. During the 2001 recession, Democrats in Congress actually demanded that the government raise taxes, abandoning both fifty years of party tradition and economic logic. The idea of a budget balanced at high employment probably remained the best approach yet devised to fiscal policy and an idea that both Democrats and Republicans would do well to revisit.

Both approaches to rescuing Social Security, Democratic and Republican, sought to assure the program's solvency without unpopular tax increases or reductions in benefits. Both were at least plausible, but they carried great risks. The Republicans would tie the solvency of the government's largest program to the stock market. Over time such investments have yielded good returns, but in the short run the market may be quite volatile. Periods of stagnation or even decline over several years have been common. What would the government do if one of these difficult periods coincided with the retirement of a large number of baby

boomers? The large drop in stock prices in 2001 and 2002 reinforced this concern. For their part, Democrats would give support for the elderly priority over almost all other government
activities; this represented the opposite of investment in the future. Their program also rested on unrealistic calculations of revenue and spending. The decline of revenue associated with the
2001 recession, tax reductions enacted by the new Bush administration in 2001, and the expenses of the War on Terror following
the September 11, 2001, attacks, each individually probably in-
validated their projections. Americans were asking the right
questions about Social Security, but they had yet to discuss realistic answers.

Health care, which faced graver problems, received less attention. After the defeat of the Clinton plan in 1994, government
and private insurers attacked the matter independently, holding
steady the portion of GDP devoted to health-care spending. But
long-term prospects were not encouraging. The aging of the
population would increase the demand for care and bankrupt
Medicare even faster than Social Security. More immediate problems had also developed. Federal restrictions on payments led
many doctors to stop accepting Medicare or Medicaid patients,
and the growing complexity of the regulations governing these
programs absorbed more and more time and staff, increasing expenses. HMOs' restrictions on treatment were unpopular, and
Congress began to seriously consider a "patients' bill of rights" to
force HMOs to provide certain services—a measure that would
almost certainly raise costs. Eager to contain outlays without
alienating patients or doctors, legislators began to contemplate
controls on the prices of drugs, on which producers enjoyed large
earnings. But profit margins on drugs were high because developing them was risky. Most research projects yielded nothing,
and profits on successful products had to finance the failures.

Controls would limit expenses but would also retard the development of new pharmaceuticals. With respect to health care, Americans were not even asking the right questions: what could the country afford and how could it limit outlays to that level?

6

The Ways of Wealth

THE AMERICAN ECONOMY changed immensely between 1945 and 2000. Gross Domestic Product quintupled, and the workforce grew to two and a half times its 1945 size. Almost every index of material well-being advanced. Goods like dishwashers and air conditioners, luxuries in 1945, were commonplace by 2000. A wide variety of new products, ranging from computers to televisions to antibiotics, became available. Average life expectancy increased from sixty-five to seventy-six years. Before World War II only the elite attended college, but by the end of the century roughly half of young people received higher education. The composition of the economy changed too. Manufacturing accounted for about 40 percent of output in 1945, but by 2000 it constituted less than 20 percent. Heavy industries like steel, machinery, and rubber, which made up the core of the American economy in 1945, were in decline by 2000. Information technology, a minor factor in 1945, was by the end of the century driving growth.

Certain key factors remained constant throughout this period, however. Capitalism reigned unchallenged. Even in the 1960s, an era of radical social change—the civil rights and women's movements—alternative economic systems received little serious attention. Political debate usually came back to the question of the source of wealth. Public investment, for instance, was an important issue from the 1940s through the 1990s, albeit in different guises. The American government remained committed to an open system of international trade and finance. The goals of the World Trade Organization, approved in 1994, and of the International Trade Organization, debated in the 1940s, were similar. The success of the former and the failure of the latter reflected changes in opinion abroad more than in Washington.

This context permitted dramatic change. The shift from mass production to (for lack of a better term) information management, which touched every aspect of the economy, offers perhaps the best example. Although historians often characterize the era between 1945 and 1973 as one of economic stability, it actually witnessed enormous upheavals: the countryside emptied out, suburbs developed, television and antibiotics became available, and income and employment grew substantially. More than any other single factor, expansion reflected broader and more intensive applications of mass-production techniques, not only to manufacturing but also to services and construction. Government policy—subsidies, regulation, and spending—guaranteed markets large enough to absorb the output of mass production, which usually required large scale to secure maximum efficiency. Greater productivity allowed steady increases in both wages and profits. Opportunities existed even for those displaced by change, like small farmers, allowing them not only to maintain but actually to improve their economic position. The vast majority enjoyed at least some of the fruits of prosperity.

Difficulties began in the 1970s not because the pace of change accelerated but because it slowed. The techniques of mass production had apparently reached a point of diminishing returns, and without higher productivity, government policies designed to create strong demand merely translated into inflation. Stagnation was unacceptable both to the American public and to U.S. business, but if they wanted growth, companies had to find new products and new ways to improve productivity. Yet no obvious way forward presented itself. Americans spent the next two decades trying to recreate conditions for steady, broad-based growth. This process entailed considerable reorganization which disrupted established patterns of doing business. Positions that had once offered security—jobs in auto plants or steel mills or in the middle management at large companies—no longer did so. Training in fields like computer programming, which barely existed in 1960, became a passport to prosperity. Those who were— either by foresight or by luck—in the forefront of change did extraordinarily well, but those who failed to move quickly enough lost ground. The intensification of foreign competition, in part a product of the American government's commitment to open trade, made the situation worse.

By the late 1990s a new system promising regular, broad-based growth had emerged—information management. It differed from mass production, however. Mass production had advanced in a linear fashion, with ever-greater standardization of products and the specialization of workers and machines allowing greater output at lower prices. In many ways a rigid system, it could co-exist with fairly rigid union contracts and government regulations. The new system followed no such steady line of advance. It did not so much supplant mass production as move beyond it, using computers to coordinate the various stages of making and delivering products ever more closely. This squeezed the "slack" out of the economic system, eliminating idle workers, inventories, and machines, and it allowed greater variation in products and maximum efficiency at lower levels of output. Information management demanded constant changes in production and delivery schedules and was incompatible with rigid union contracts or government regulation. Such rules had to become more flexible, dictating outcomes (wages, pollution levels) rather than procedures (work rules, pollution-control systems).

Government reforms during the last quarter of the twentieth century accommodated and even encouraged this development. Politicians understood the direction of change no better than anyone else, but they did realize that, with the way forward unclear, government had to encourage innovation. Deregulation, tax reduction, changes in the enforcement of labor and anti-trust laws, and the Clinton administration's budget program all reflected this sentiment. These reforms represented a major shift in economic policy. From the 1930s through the 1960s economic policy had sought to smooth out the rough edges of capitalism by limiting destructive competition, protecting workers, and stabilizing demand. Starting in the late 1970s, government policy increasingly sought to hone the cutting edge of the capitalist system, encouraging innovation, investment, and risk-taking.

Ultimately a country's wealth depends not on what it has but on what it is. Natural resources play out, factories depreciate, and technology becomes obsolete. To prosper over generations, a country must continually reorganize its economy, devising new products and new ways of making and marketing existing ones. This is often disconcerting and painful, but it represents the only alternative to economic stagnation. Dynamic societies need innovations, the vast majority of which originate with entrepreneurs in the private sector. But entrepreneurs are products of their environment. They will succeed only if the larger society provides encouragement, status, and resources (markets, labor, and capital), and tolerates the dislocations that their efforts sometimes bring. During the second half of the twentieth century, the United States did all of this as well as any nation on earth.

A Note on Sources

INTELLECTUALLY this book draws heavily on Joseph Schumpeter's *Capitalism, Socialism, and Democracy* (New York, 1942) and, to a lesser degree, on Theodore Rosenof's *Economics in the Long Run: New Deal Theorists and Their Legacies, 1933–1993* (Chapel Hill, 1997).

The U.S. Bureau of the Census's *Historical Statistics of the United States, Colonial Times to 1870, Bicentennial Edition* (Washington, D.C., 1975) and annual *Statistical Abstract of the United States,* as well as the Council of Economic Advisers' annual *Economic Report of the President of the United States,* contain extensive statistics on the American economy over the last sixty years. The *Wall Street Journal,* the *New York Times,* the *Economist, Fortune,* and *Business Week* provided good coverage of the American economy over this period.

Alfred Chandler's "Competitive Performance of U.S. Industrial Enterprises Since the Second World War," *Business History Review* 68 (1994), Thomas McCraw's *American Business, 1920–2000: How It Worked* (Wheeling, Ill., 2000), Michael French's *U.S. Economic History Since 1945* (New York, 1997), Robert M. Collins's *More: The Politics of Economic Growth in Postwar America* (New York, 2000), Louis Galambos and Joseph Pratt's *The Rise of the Corporate Commonwealth: United States Business and Public Policy in the Twentieth Century* (New York, 1998), and Herbert Stein's *Presidential Economics: The Making of Economic Policy from Roosevelt to Clinton* (New York, 1994) examine the development of the American economy after 1945.

Valuable studies of specific economic topics during the period since 1945 include Daniel Nelson's *Shifting Fortunes: The Rise and Decline of American Labor, from the 1820s to the Present* (Chicago, 1997), the U.S. Census Bureau's *The Changing Shape of the Nation's*

Income Distribution, 1947–1998 (Washington, D.C., 2000), Moses Abramovitz and Paul David's *Two Centuries of American Macroeconomic Growth: From Exploitation of Resource Abundance to Knowledge-Driven Development* (Palo Alto, 2001), Iwan Morgan's *Deficit Government: Taxing and Spending in Modern America* (Chicago, 1995), Robert Solomon's *The International Monetary System, 1945–81: An Insider's View* (New York, 1982), Donald Kettl's *Leadership at the Fed* (New Haven, 1986), John Wooley's *Monetary Politics: The Federal Reserve and the Politics of Monetary Policy* (New York, 1984), Andrea Gabor's *The Capitalist Philosophers: The Geniuses of Modern Business—Their Lives, Times, and Ideas* (New York, 2000), Hugh Rockoff's *Drastic Measures: A History of Wage and Price Controls in the United States* (New York, 1984), Richard Vietor's *Contrived Competition: Regulation and Deregulation in America* (Cambridge, Mass., 1994), Thomas McCraw's *Prophets of Regulation: Charles Frances Adams, Louis D. Brandeis, James M. Landis, and Alfred E. Kahn* (Cambridge, Mass., 1986), and Daniel Yergin's majestic *The Prize: The Epic Quest for Oil, Money, and Power* (New York, 1992).

General surveys that discuss economic issues intelligently include James Patterson's *Grand Expectations: The United States, 1945–1974* (New York, 1996), Alonzo Hamby's *Beyond the New Deal: Harry S Truman and American Liberalism* (New York, 1973), Charles Alexander's *Holding the Line: The Eisenhower Era, 1952–1961* (Bloomington, Ind., 1975), Stephen Ambrose's *Eisenhower: The President* (New York, 1984), William L. O'Neill's *Coming Apart: An Informal History of America in the 1960s* (Chicago, 1971), Allen Matusow's *The Unraveling of America: A History of Liberalism in the 1960s* (New York, 1984), and Ambrose's *Nixon: Triumph of a Politician, 1962–1972* (New York, 1989) and *Nixon: Ruin and Recovery, 1973–1990* (New York, 1991).

Robert M. Collins's *The Business Response to Keynes, 1929–1964* (New York, 1981), Edward Flash's *Economic Advice and Presidential Leadership: The Council of Economic Advisers* (New York, 1965), and Herbert Stein's *The Fiscal Revolution in America* (Washington, D.C.,

1969) examine the development of economic thought and policy after World War II. Richard N. Gardner's *Sterling-Dollar Diplomacy: Anglo-American Collaboration in the Reconstruction of Multilateral Trade* (Oxford, England, 1956) and Alan Milward's *The Reconstruction of Western Europe, 1945–1951* (London, 1984) discuss the revival of the international economy after World War II. John Kenneth Galbraith's *The Affluent Society* (New York, 1958) is the best liberal critique of the postwar economy. James Brooks's *The Go-Go Years* (New York, 1973) examines financial markets in the 1960s while John Love's *McDonald's: Behind the Arches* (New York, 1986) offers a perspective on the growth of the service economy. Allen Matusow's *Nixon's Economy: Booms, Busts, Dollars, and Votes* (Lawrence, Kans., 1998), James A. Reichley's *Conservatives in an Age of Change: The Nixon and Ford Administrations* (Washington, D.C., 1981), and Wyatt Wells's *Economist in an Uncertain World: Arthur F. Burns and the Federal Reserve, 1970–1978* (New York, 1994) all chronicle the economic policies of the Nixon and Ford administrations.

Books describing the economic crises of the 1970s include Martin Feldstein, ed., *The American Economy in Transition* (Chicago, 1980) and Alan Blinder, *Economic Policy and the Great Stagflation* (New York, 1979). David Halberstam's *The Reckoning* (New York, 1986) and William Greider's *Secrets of the Temple* (New York, 1987) offer a more journalistic but still valuable perspective on these events. Thomas Friedman's *The Lexus and the Olive Tree* (New York, 2000) is an eloquent brief for globalization. Alfred Chandler's *Inventing the Electronic Century: The Epic Story of the Consumer Electronics and Computer Industries* (New York, 2001) is a thorough, scholarly history of the development of "high technology" industry.

Index

A NOTE ON THE AUTHOR

Wyatt Wells is associate professor of history at Auburn University Montgomery. Born in Nashville, Tennessee, he studied at Vanderbilt University and the University of North Carolina at Chapel Hill, where he received a Ph.D. He has been a Newcomen Fellow at the Harvard Business School and a Fulbright Fellow, and an assistant editor of the Andrew Jackson Papers. His other books include *Economist in an Uncertain World: Arthur Burns and the Federal Reserve, 1970–1978*, and *Antitrust and the Formation of the Postwar World*. He is married and lives in Montgomery, Alabama.